This Book Belongs to

_ _ _ _ _ _ _ _ _ _ _ _ _ _ _ _ _ _

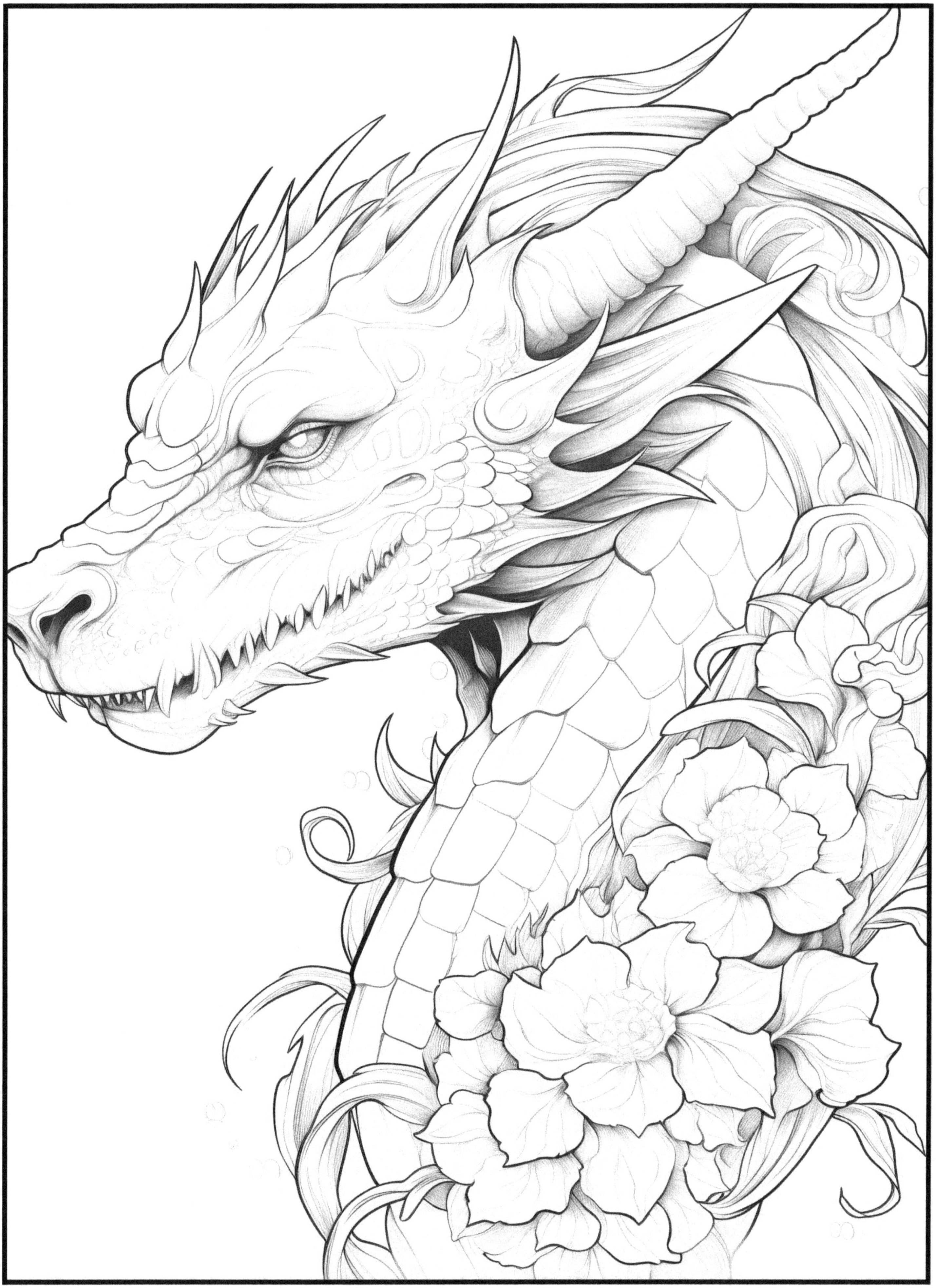

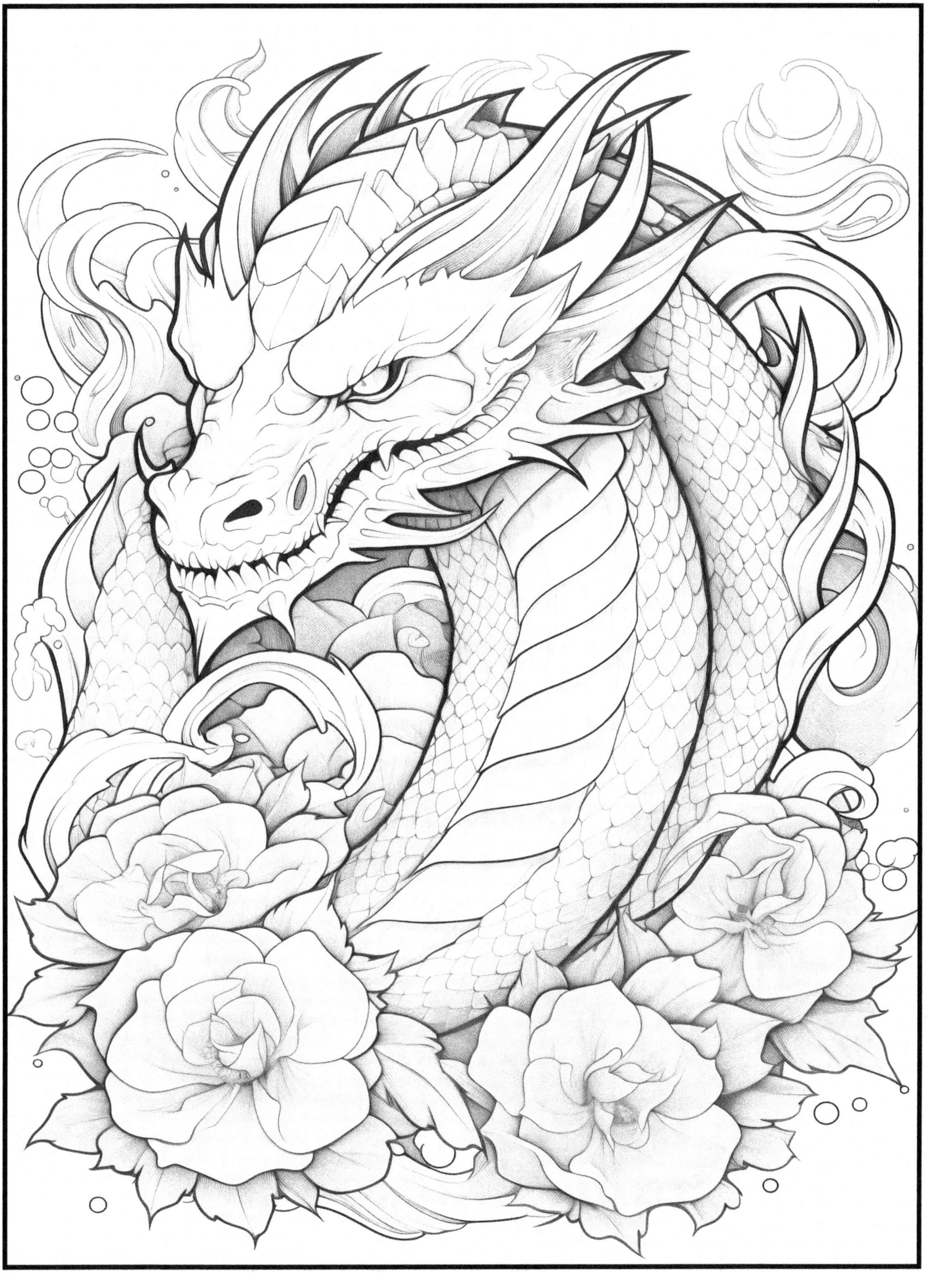

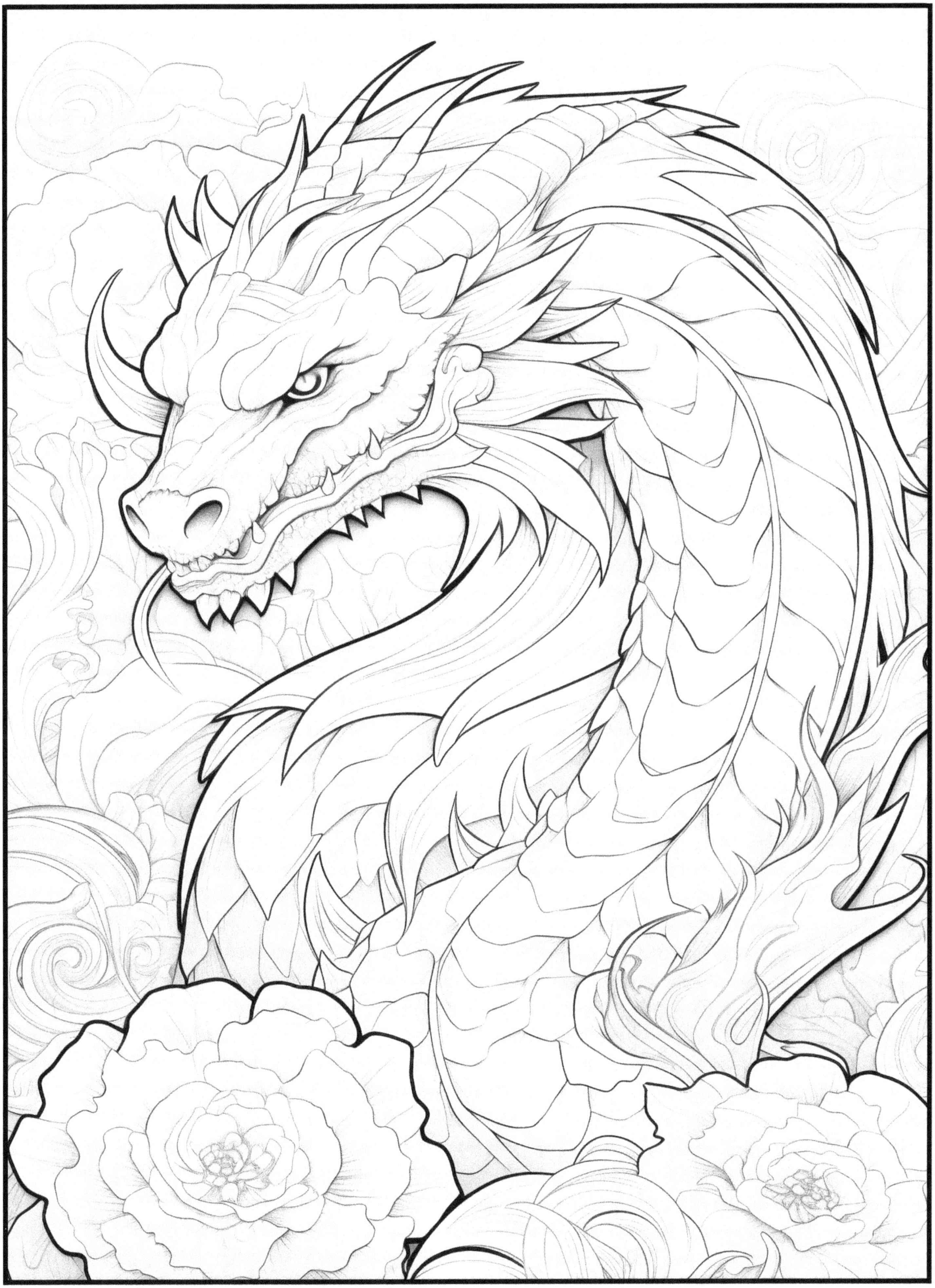

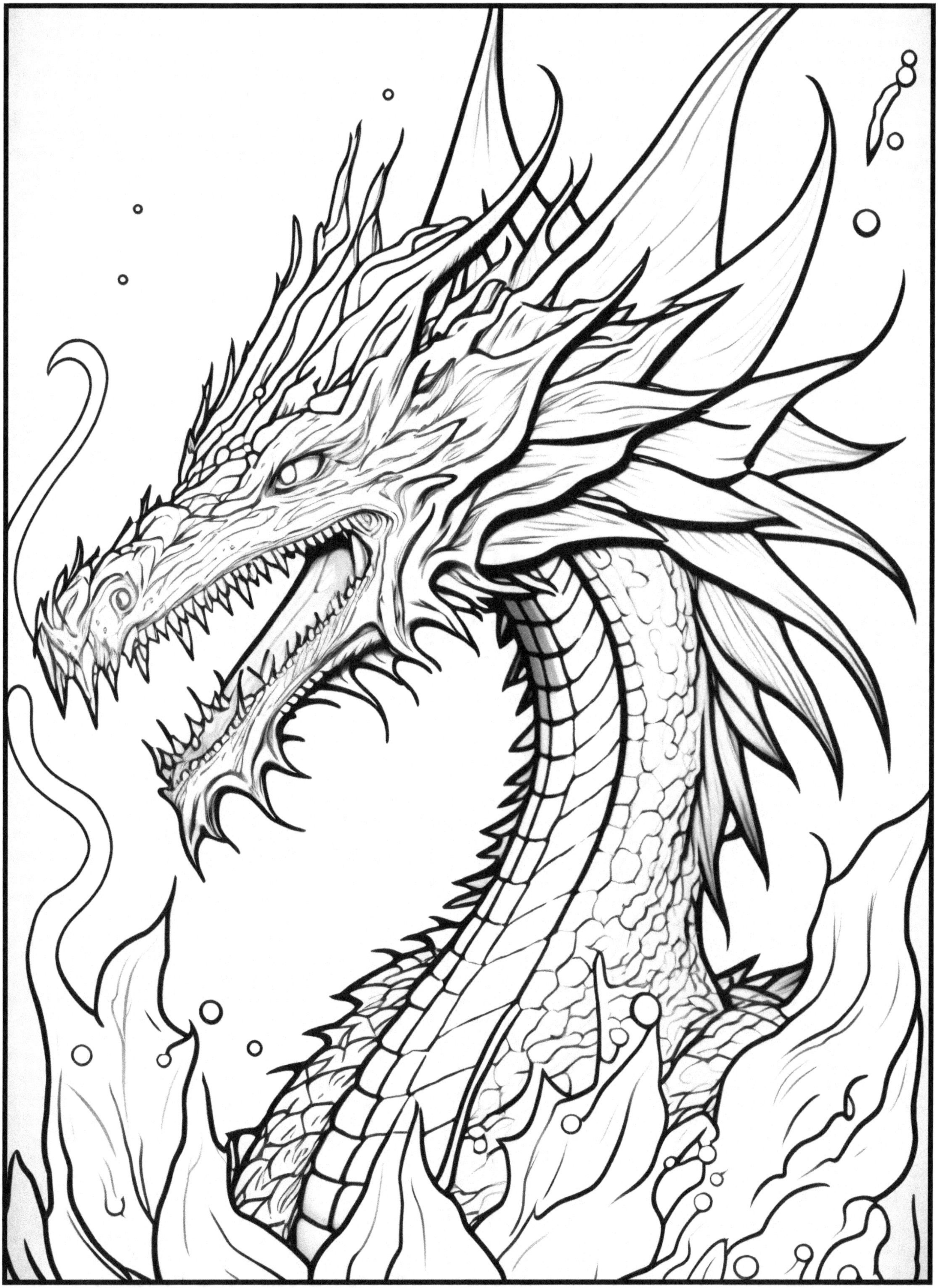

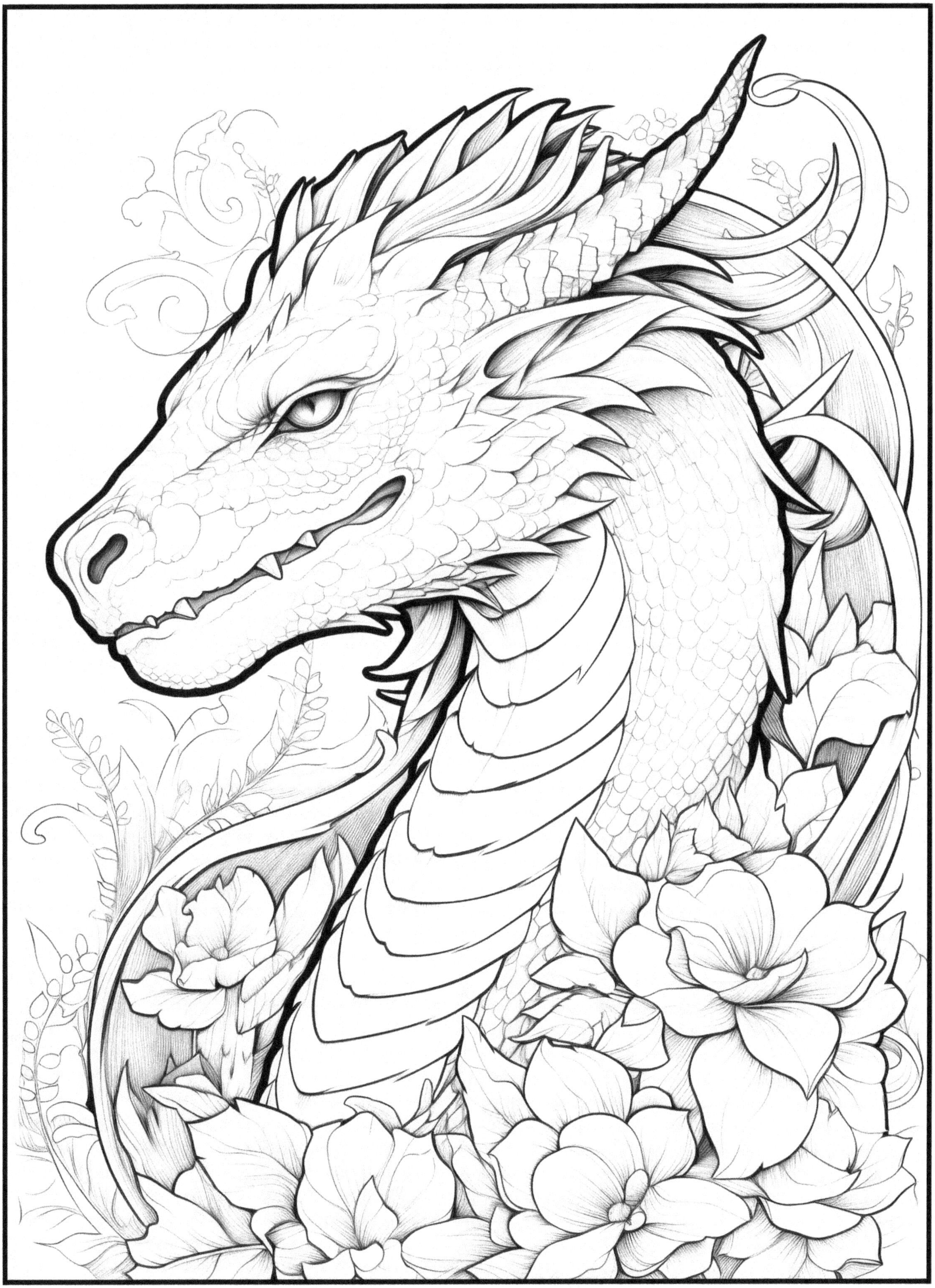

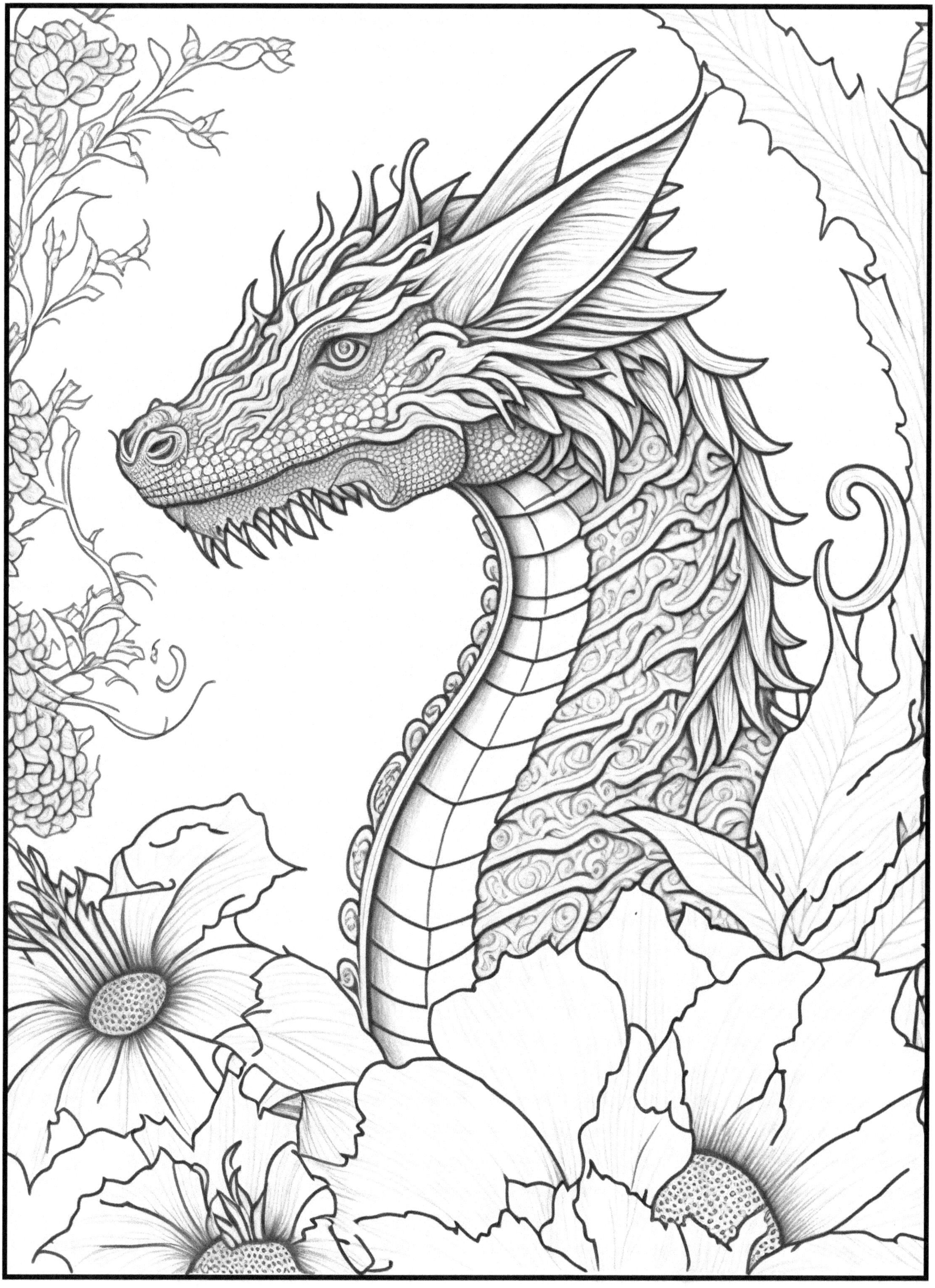

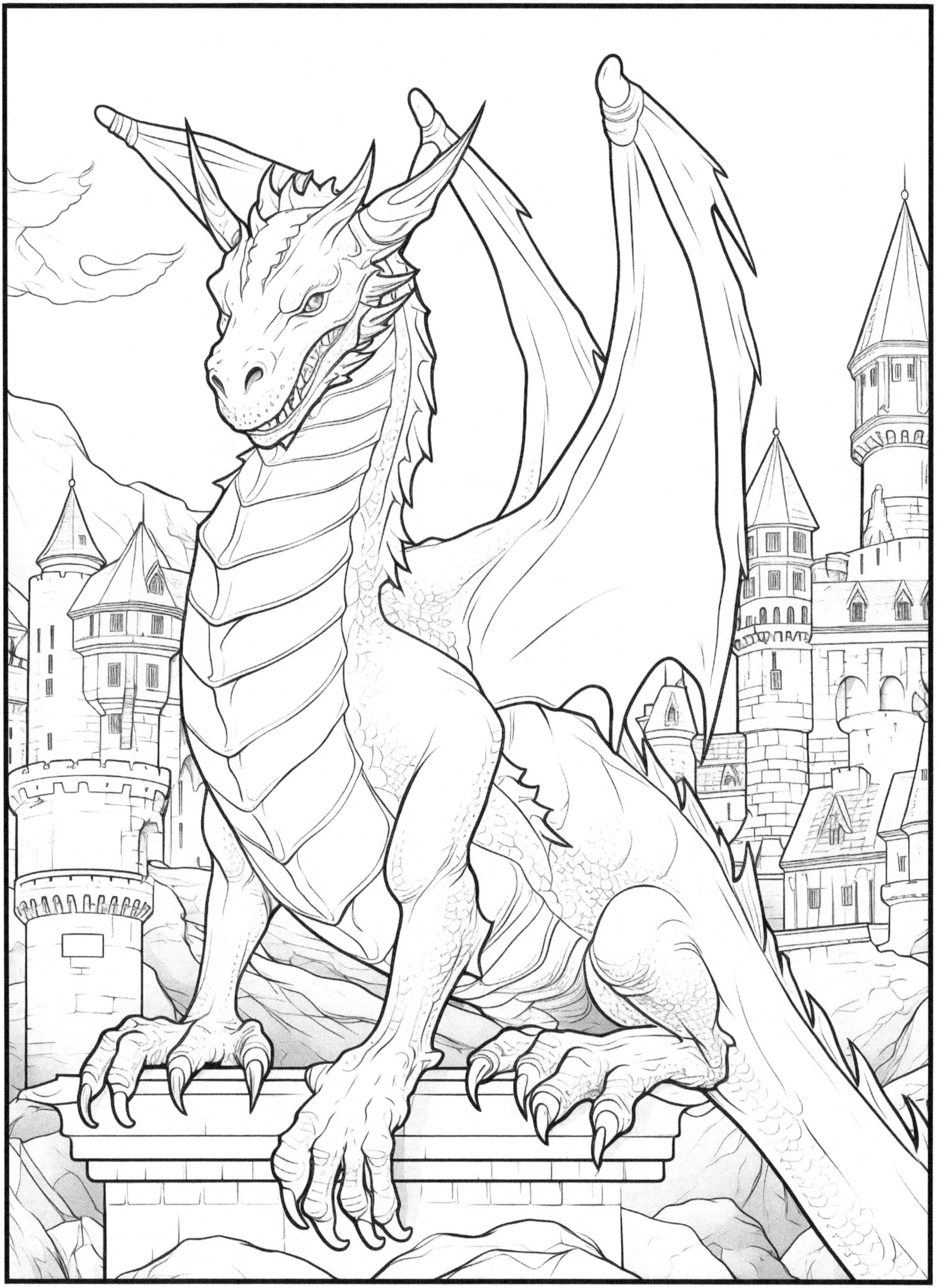

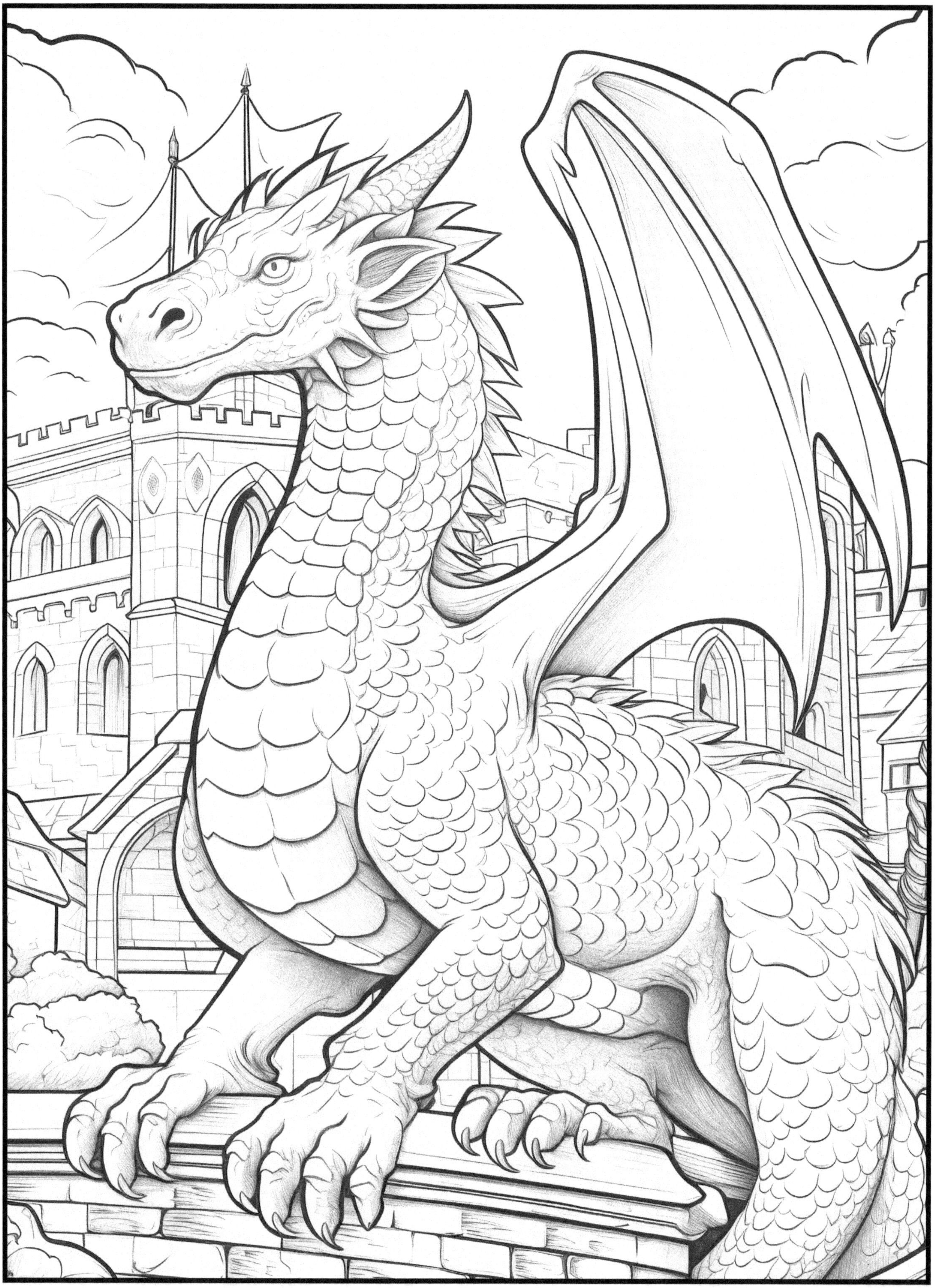

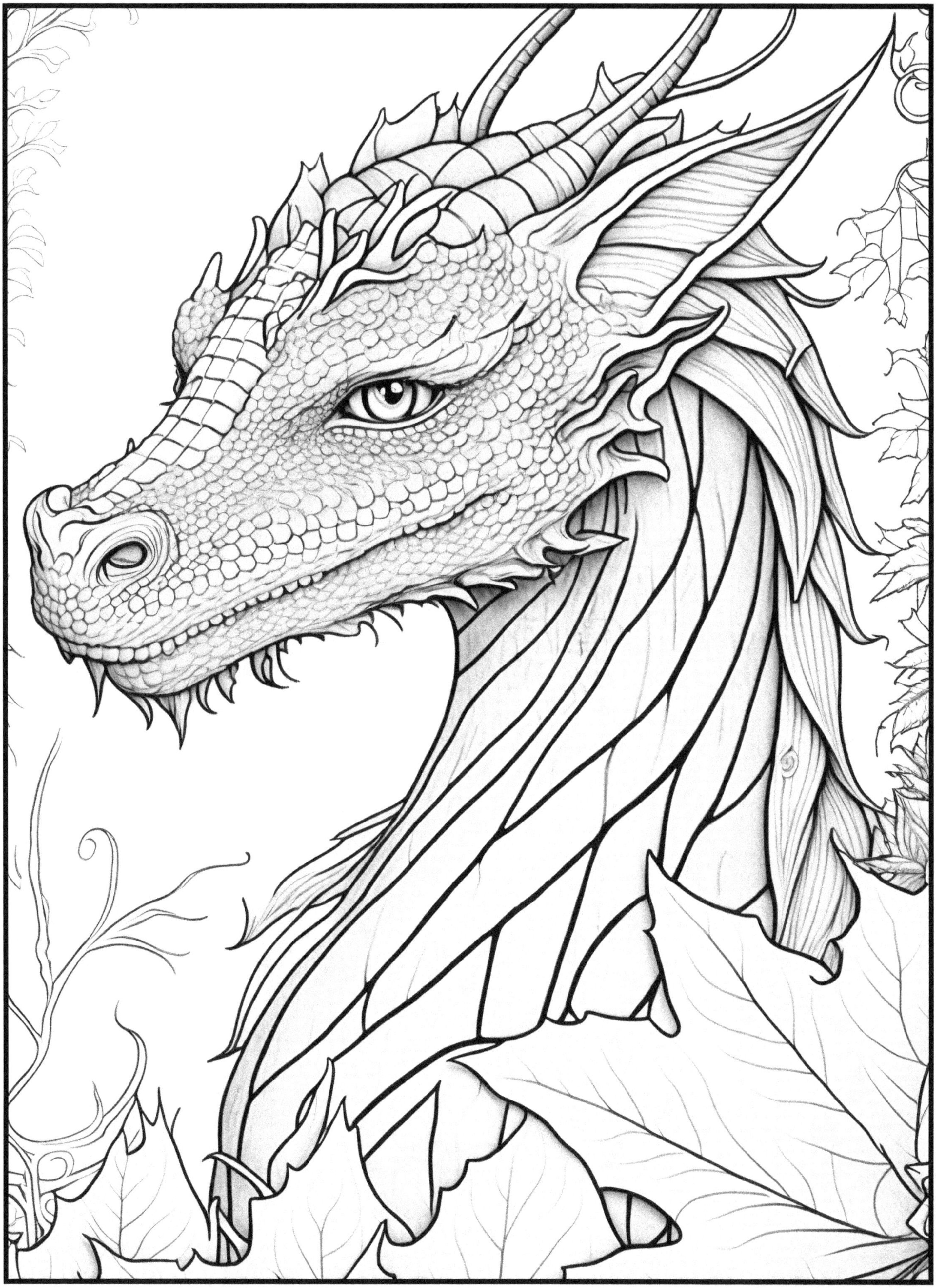

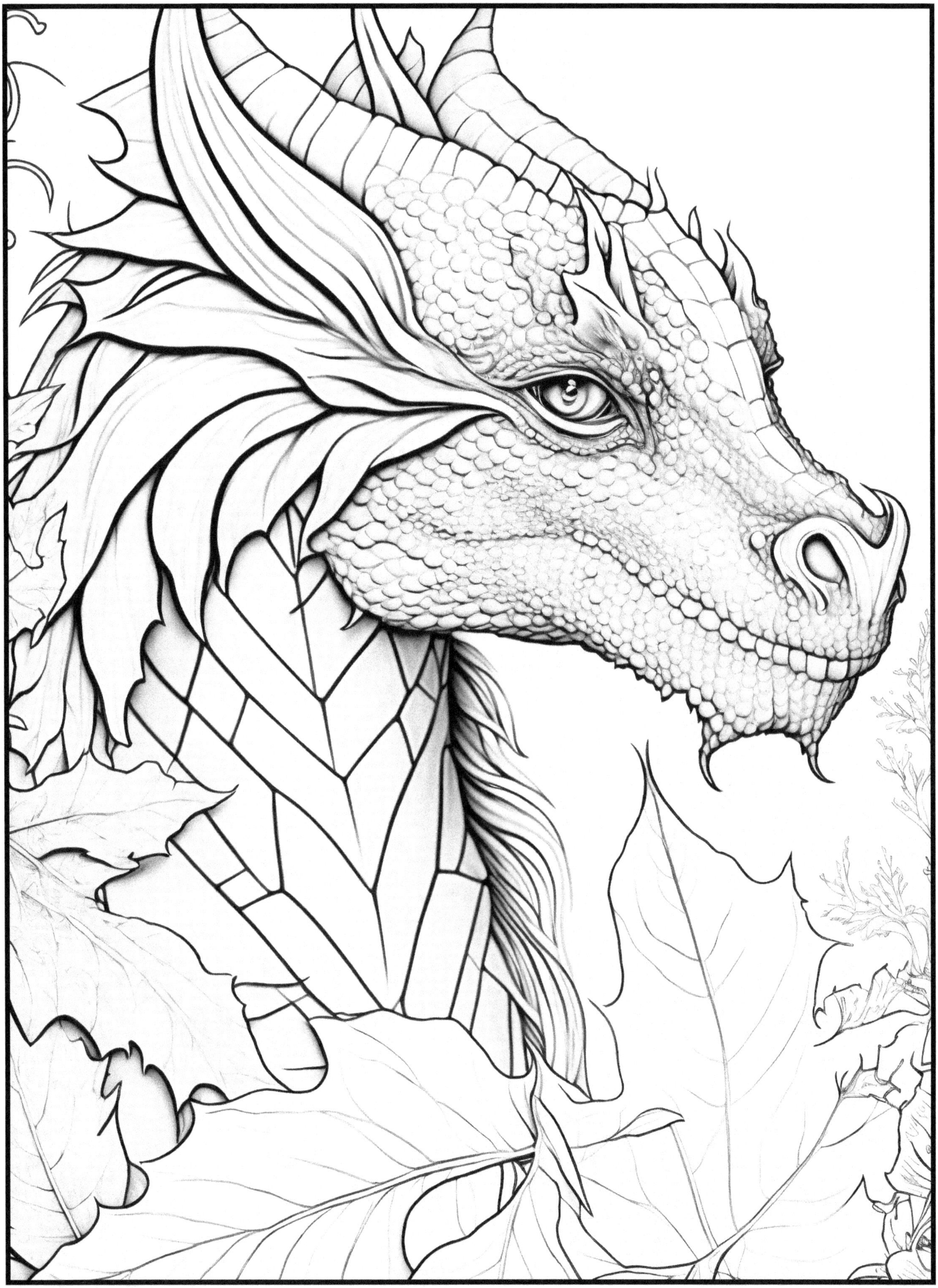

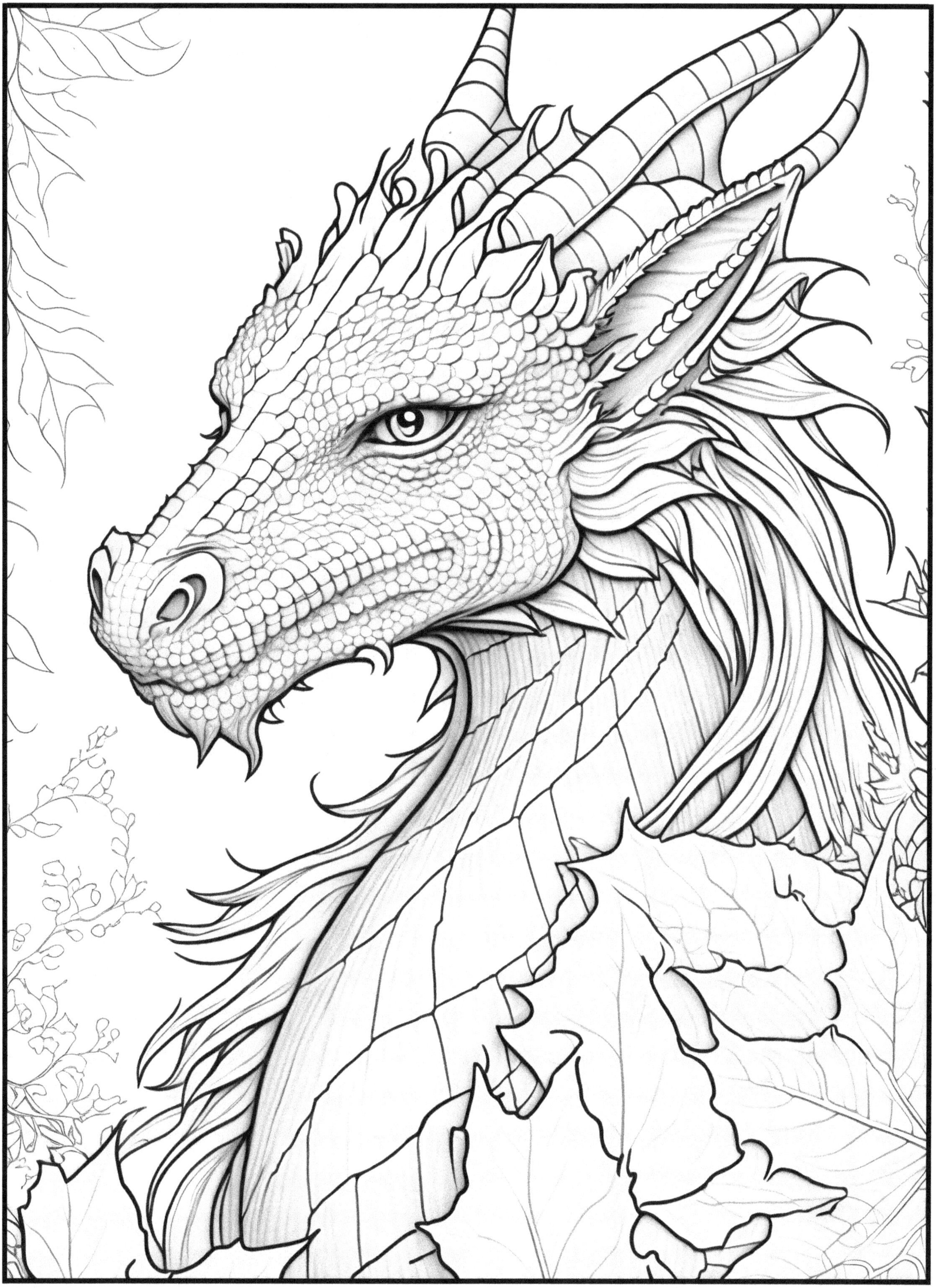

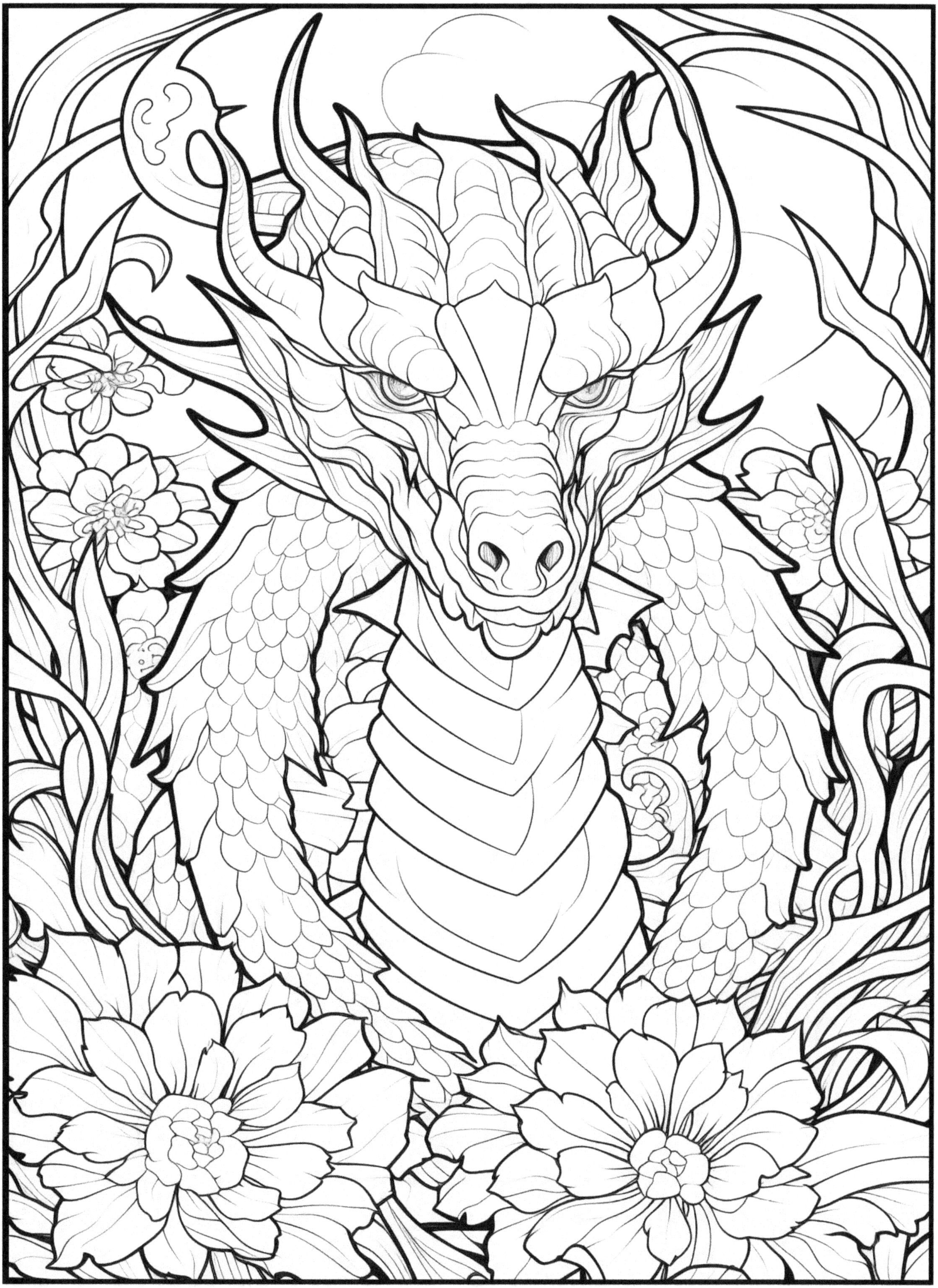

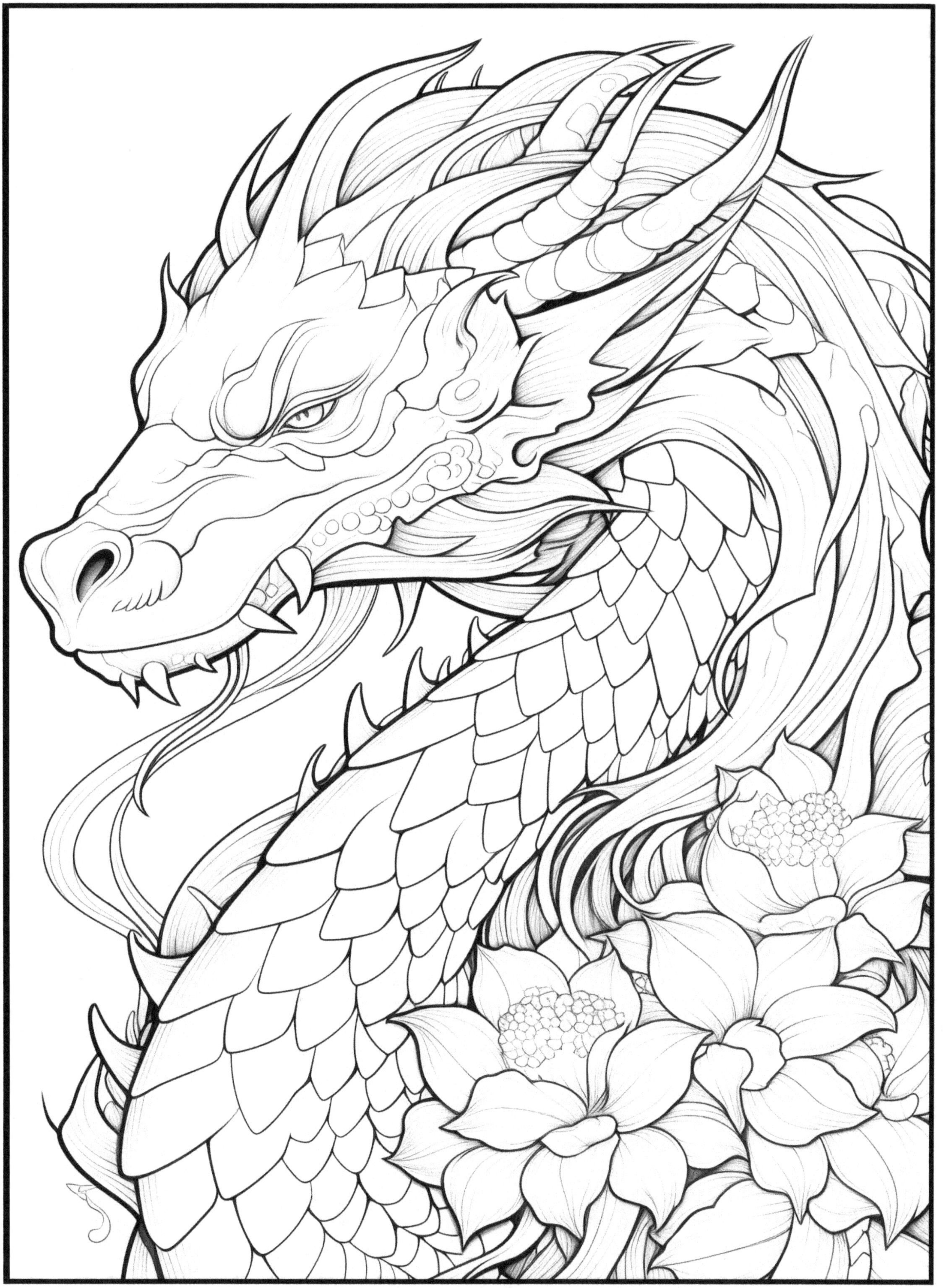

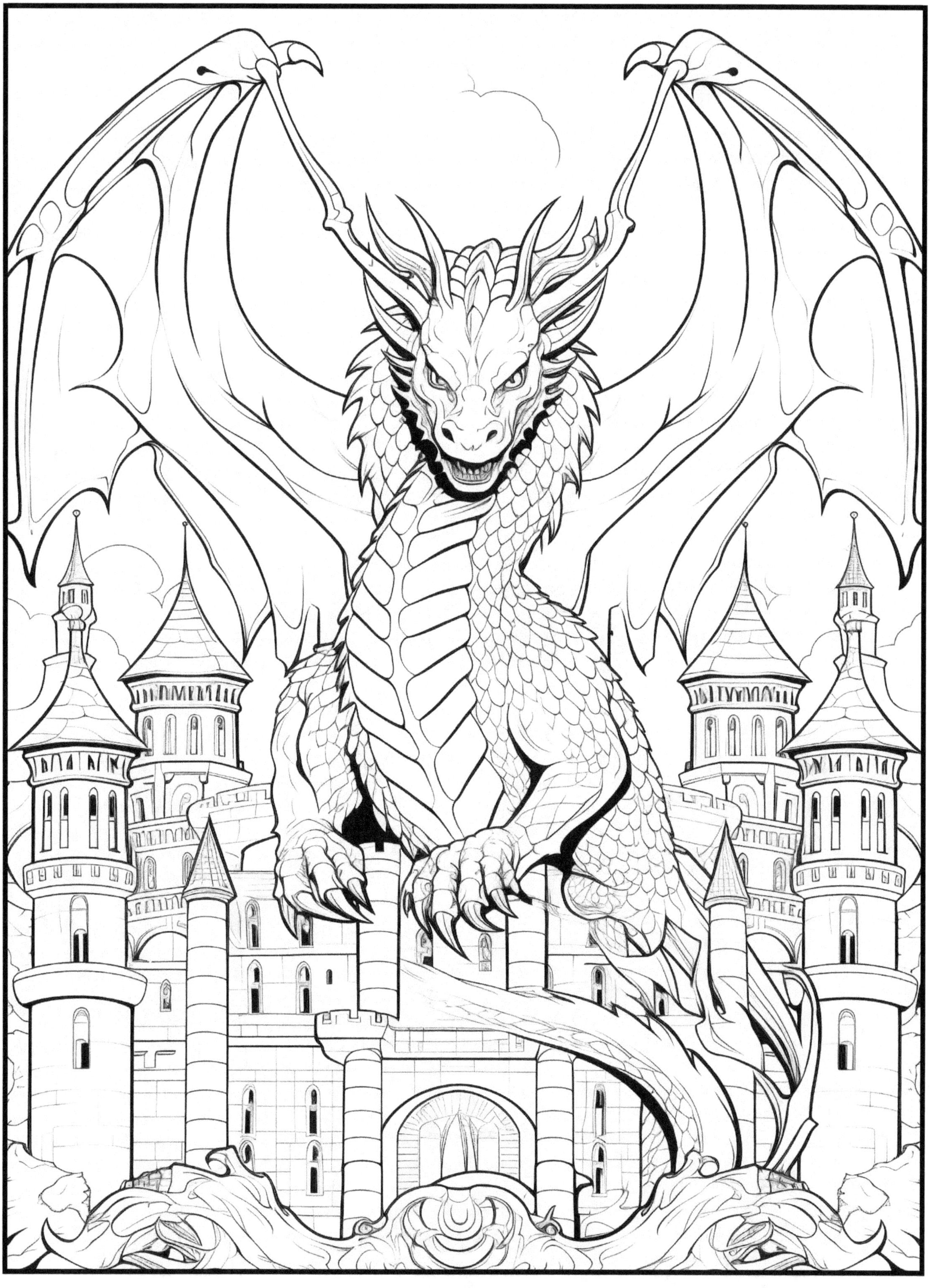

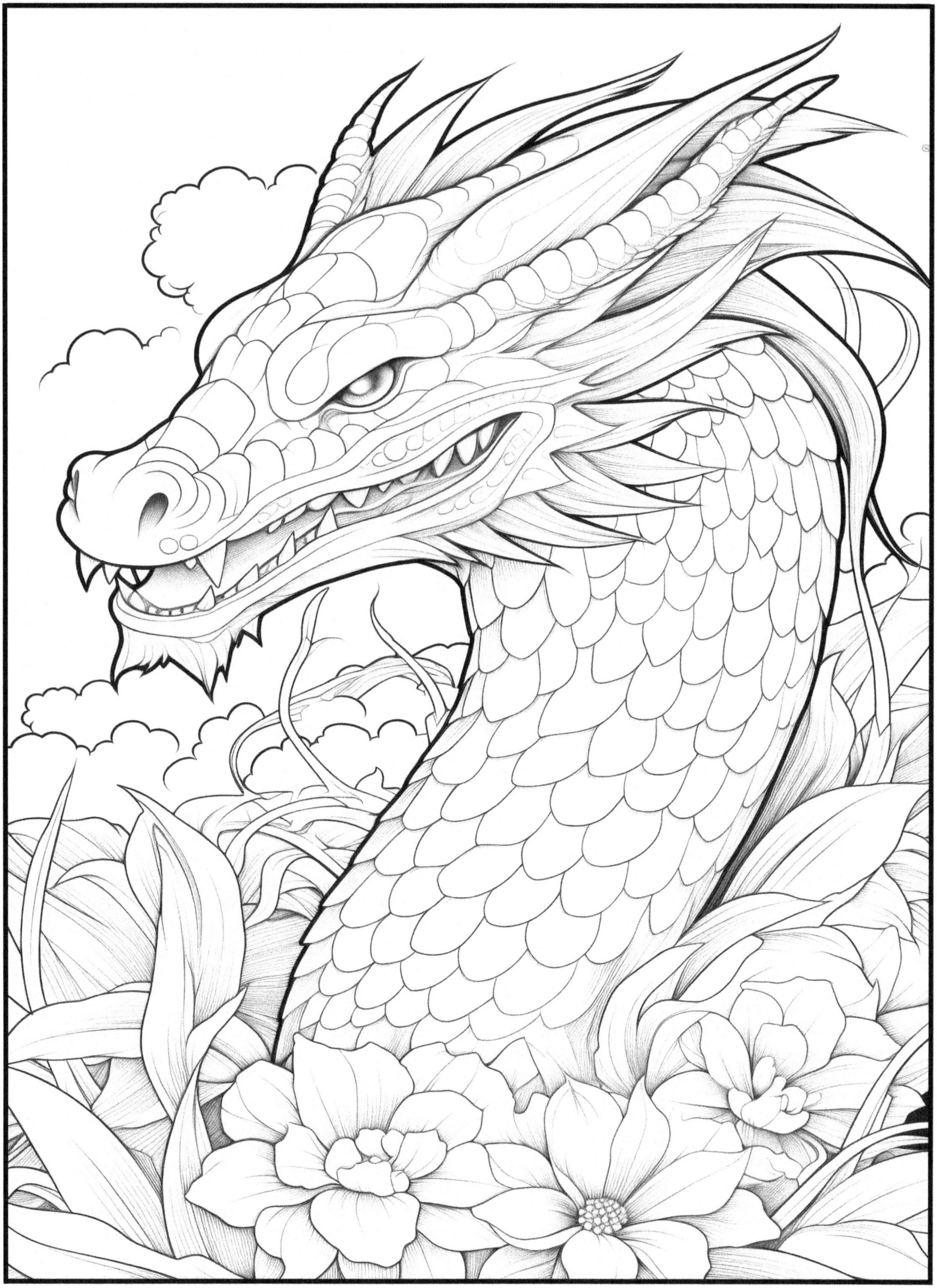

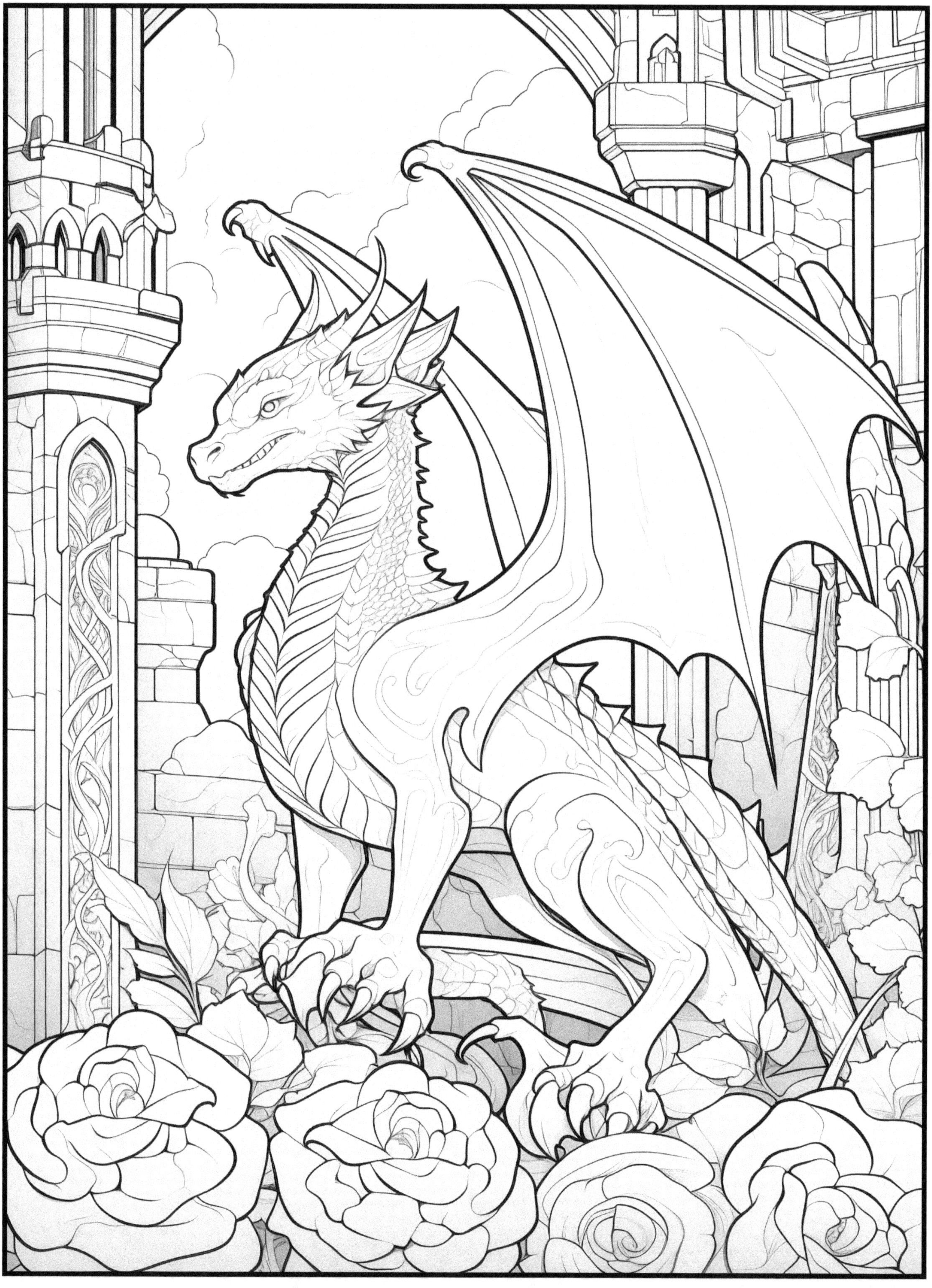

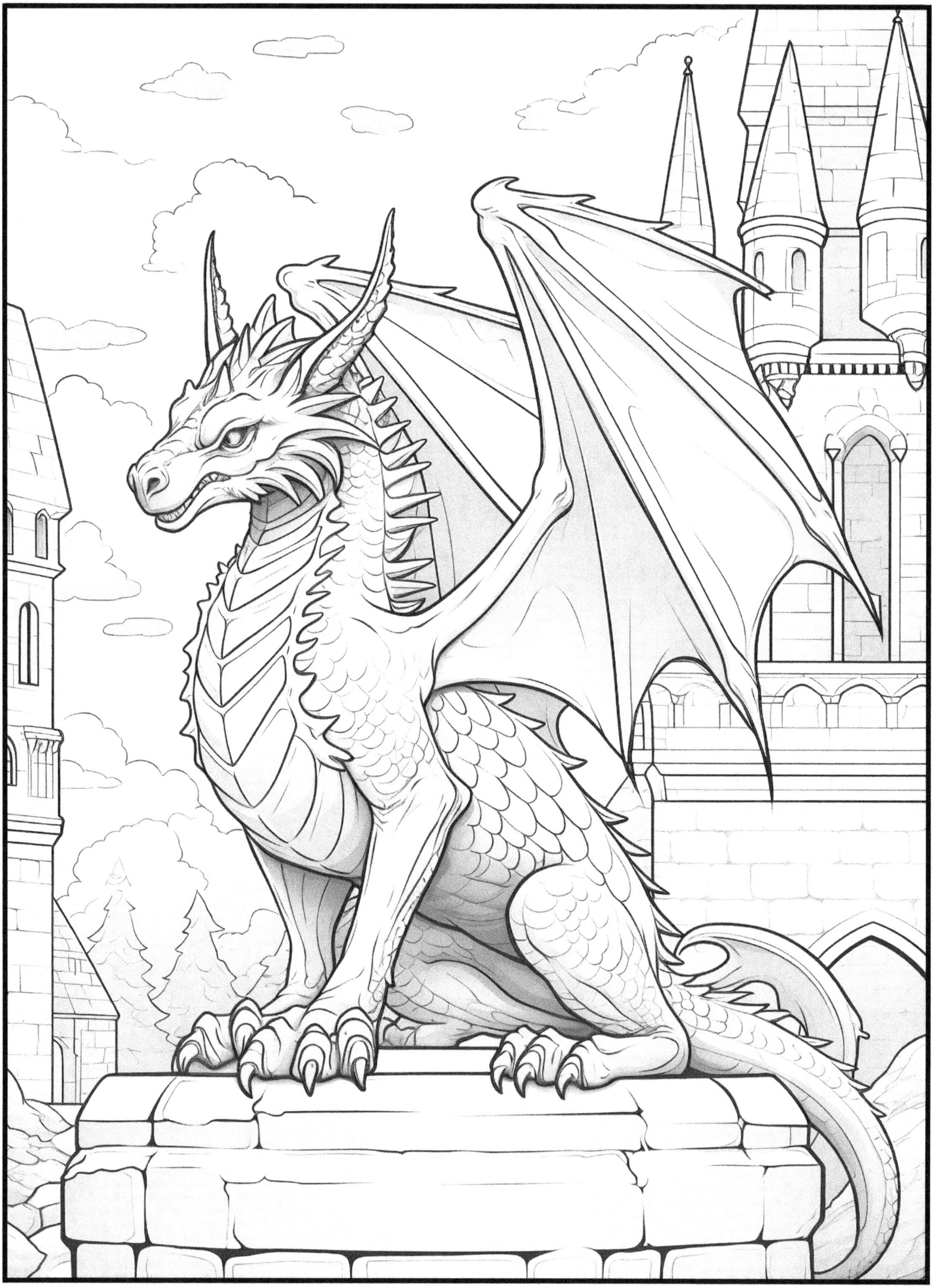

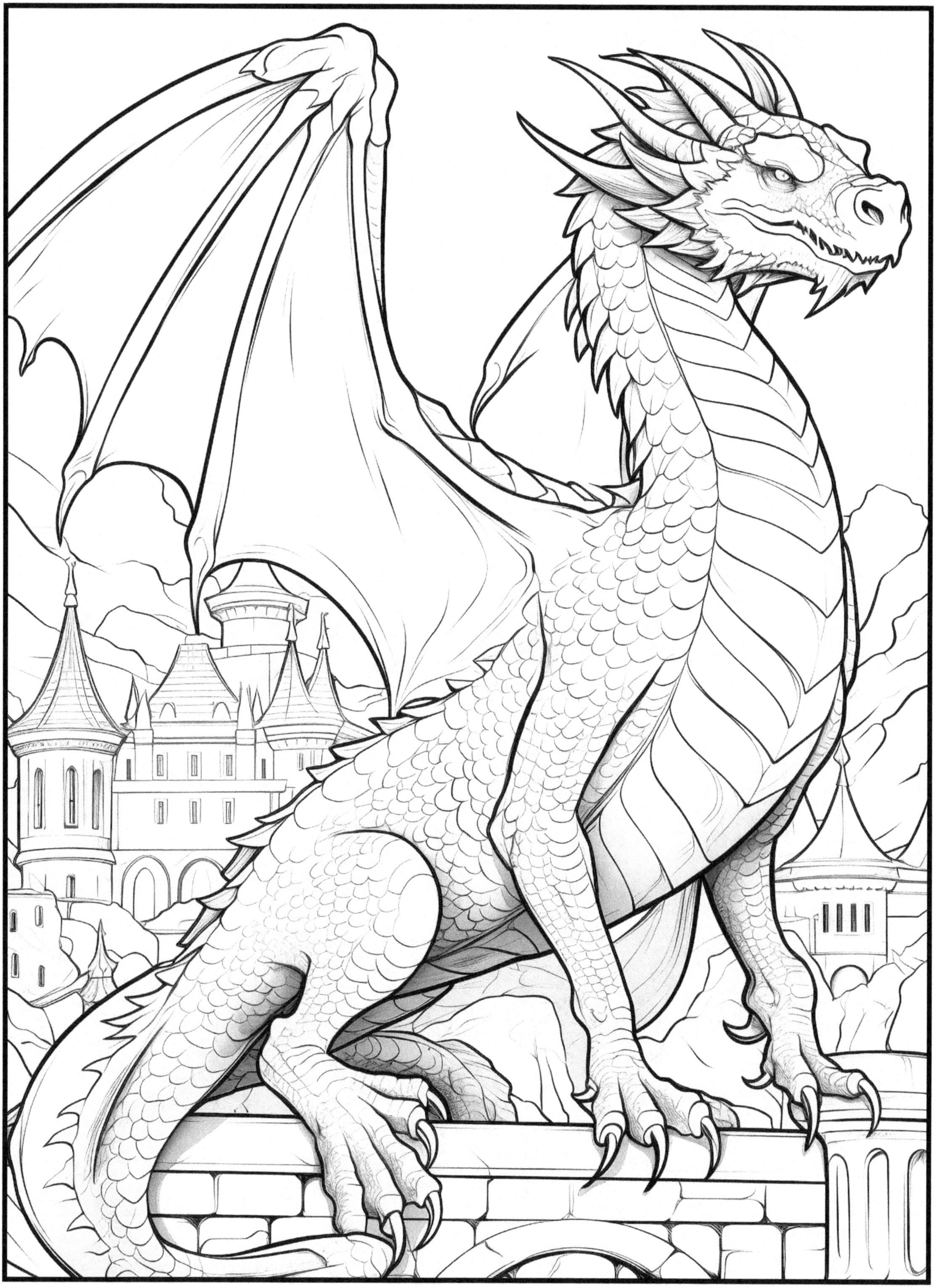

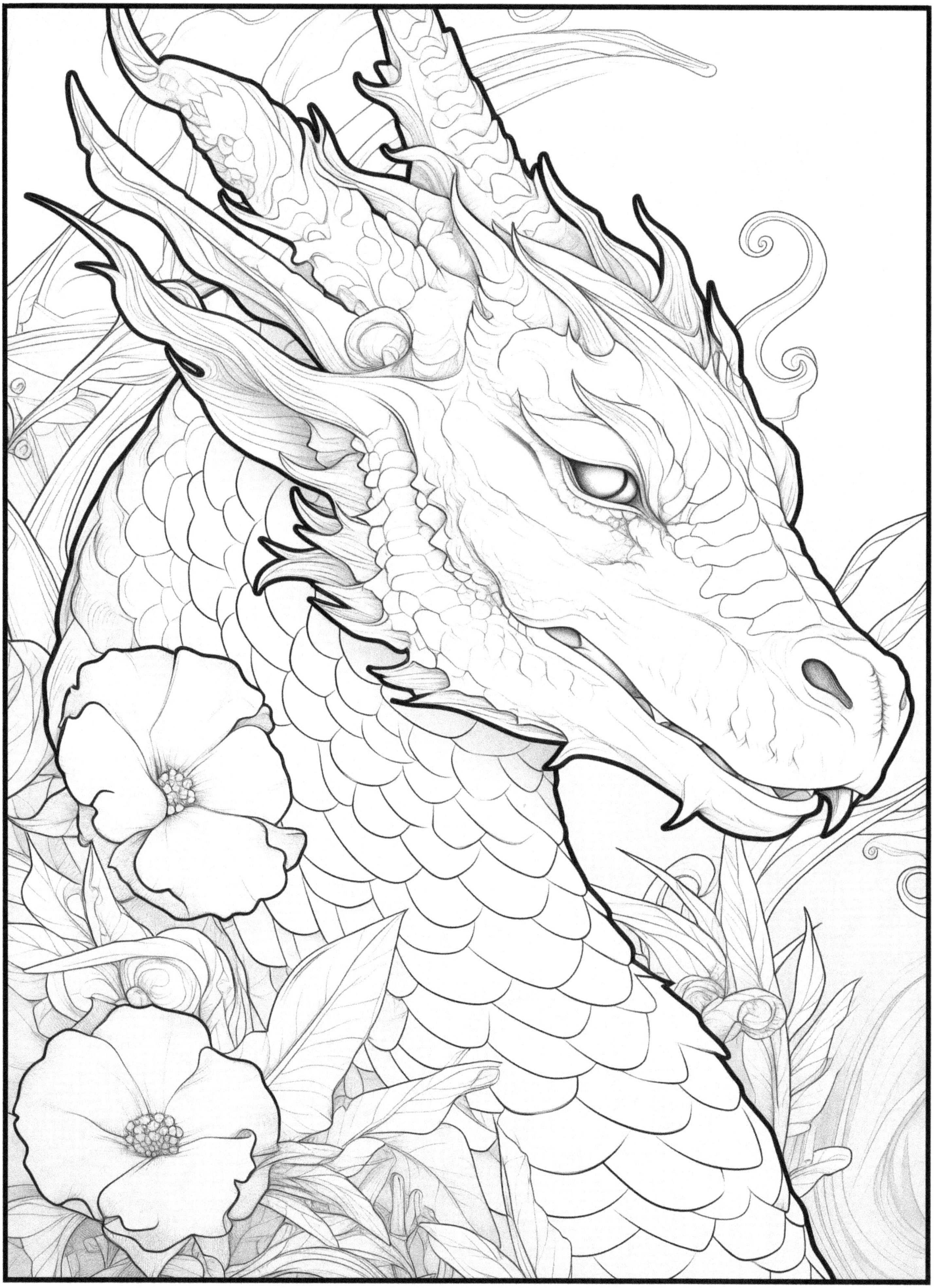

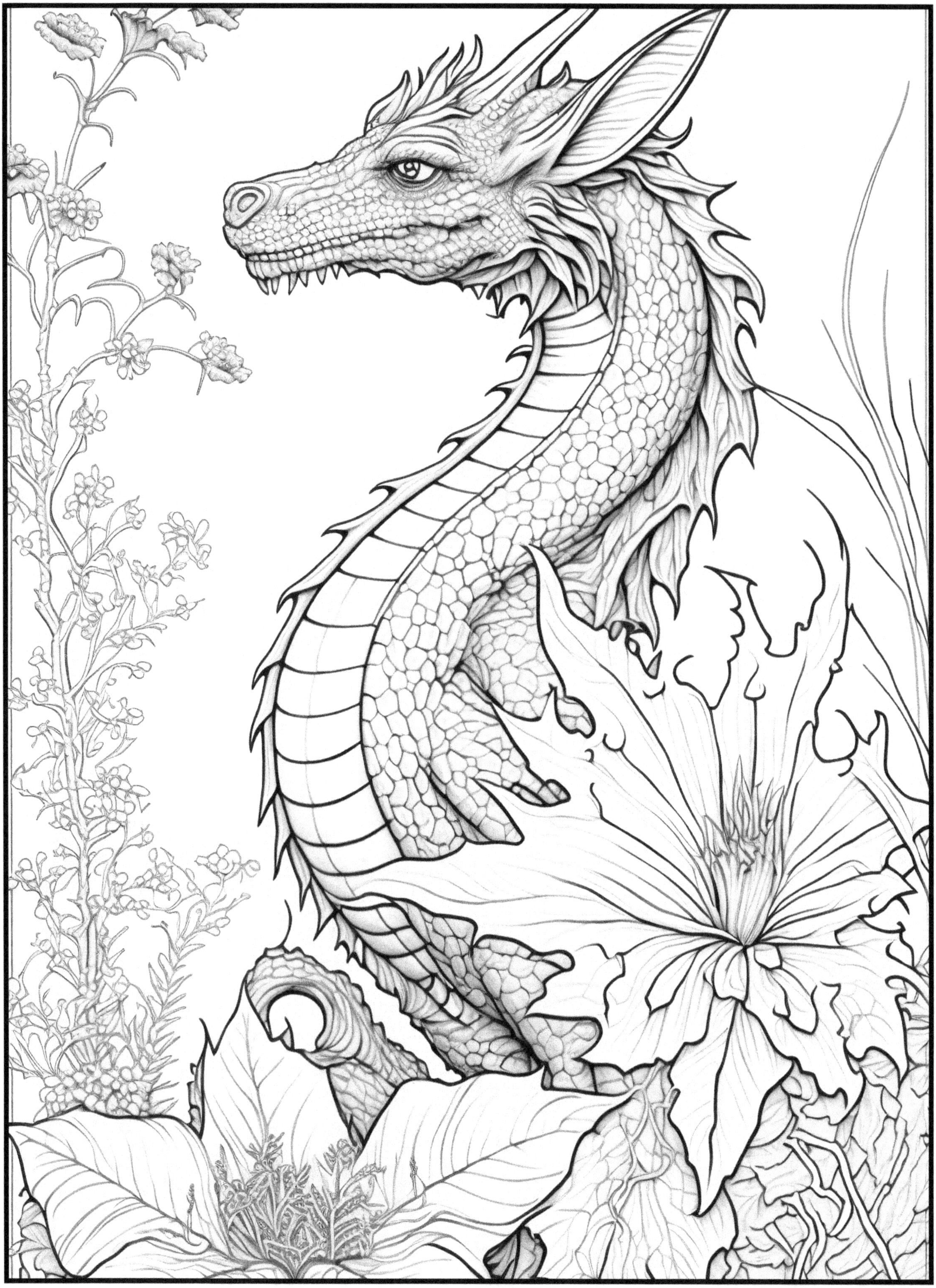

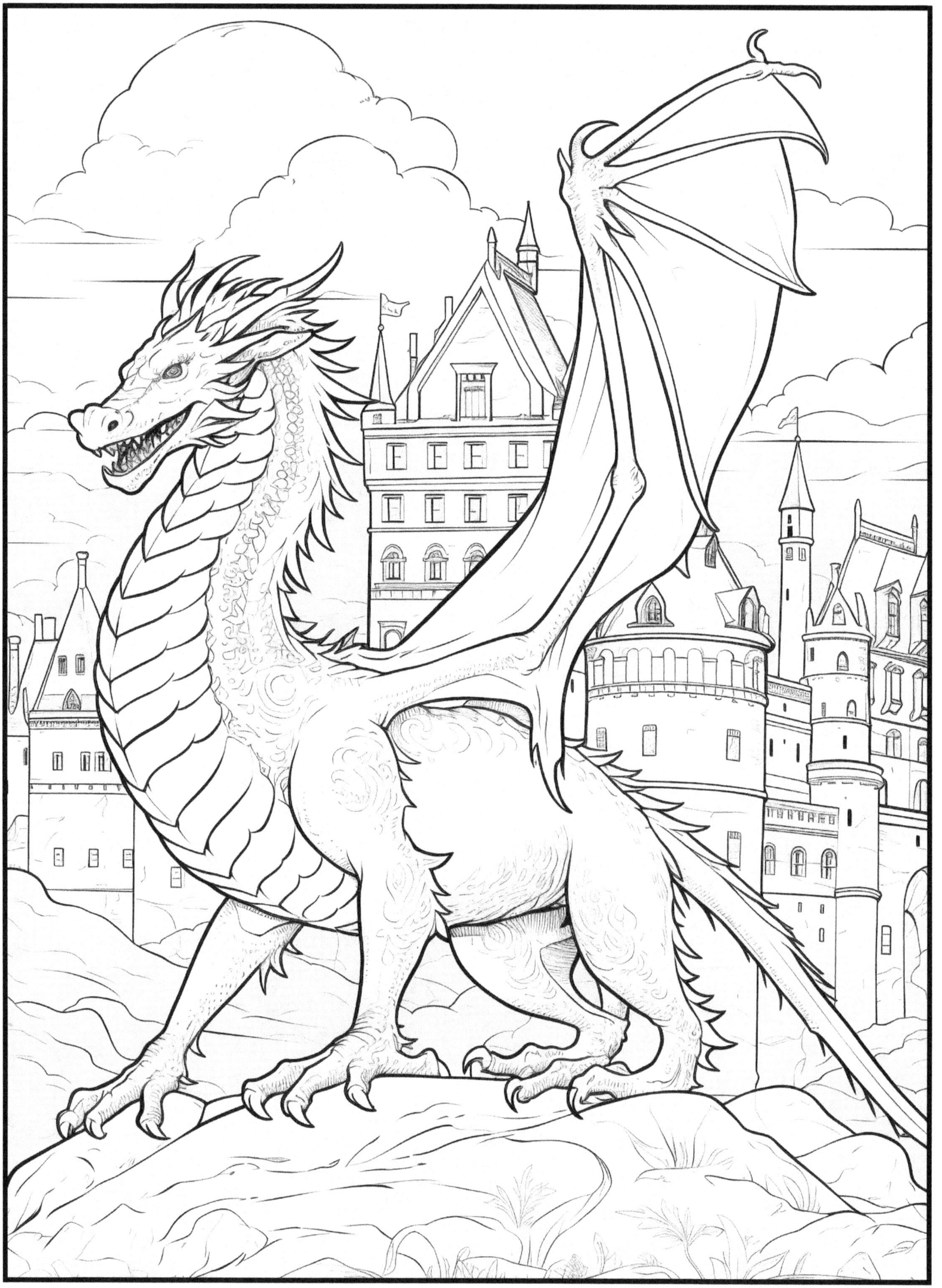

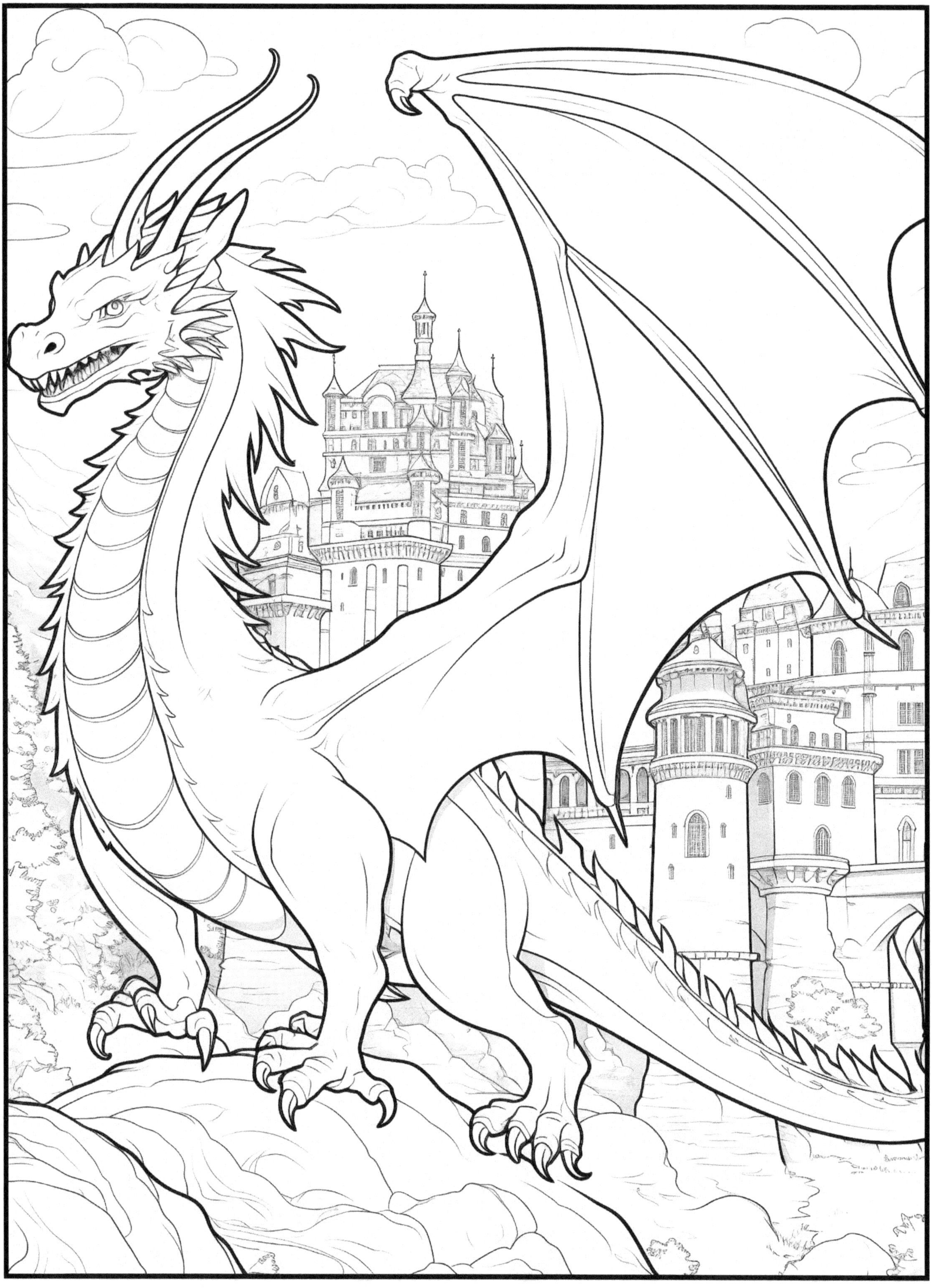

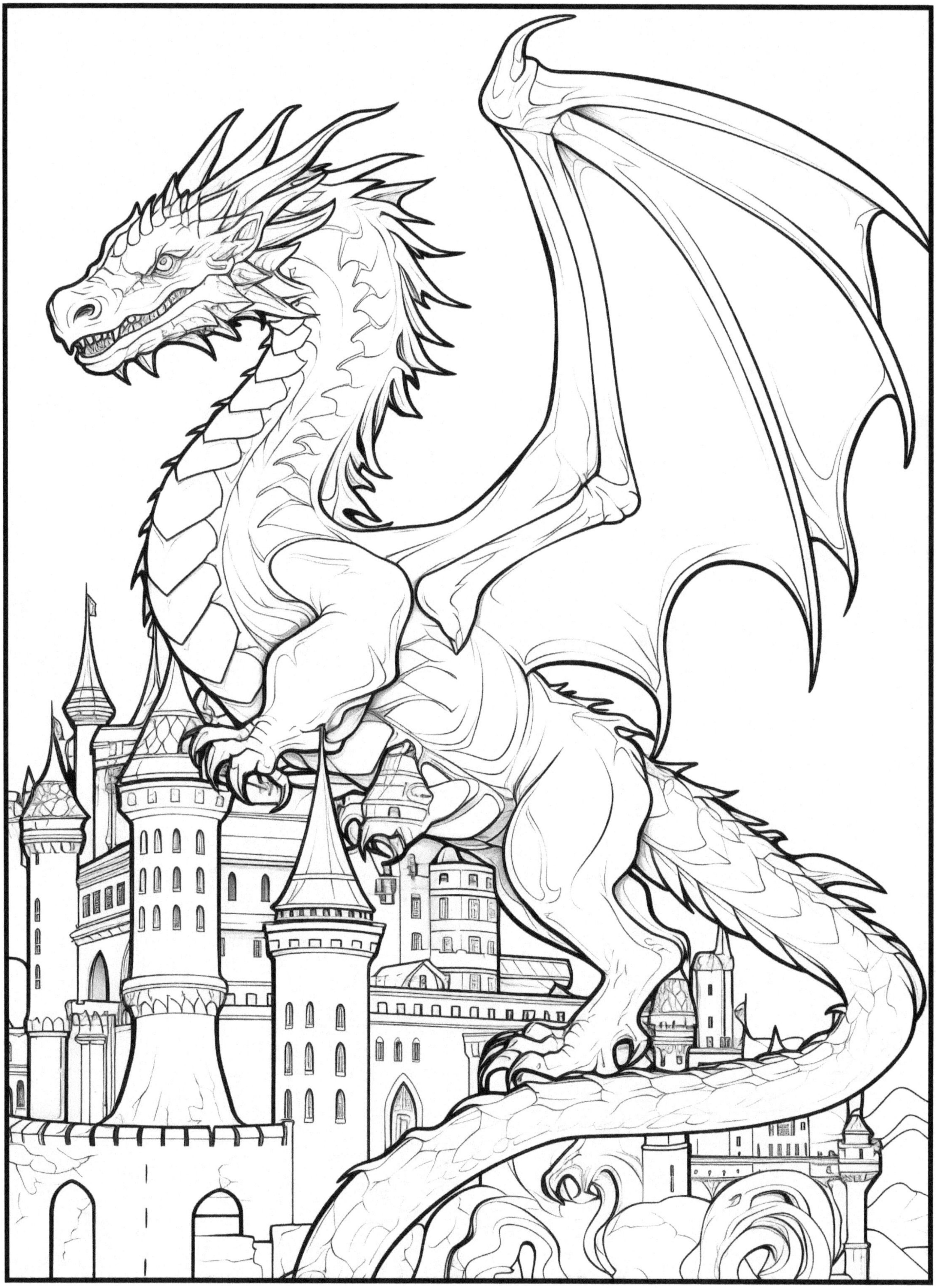

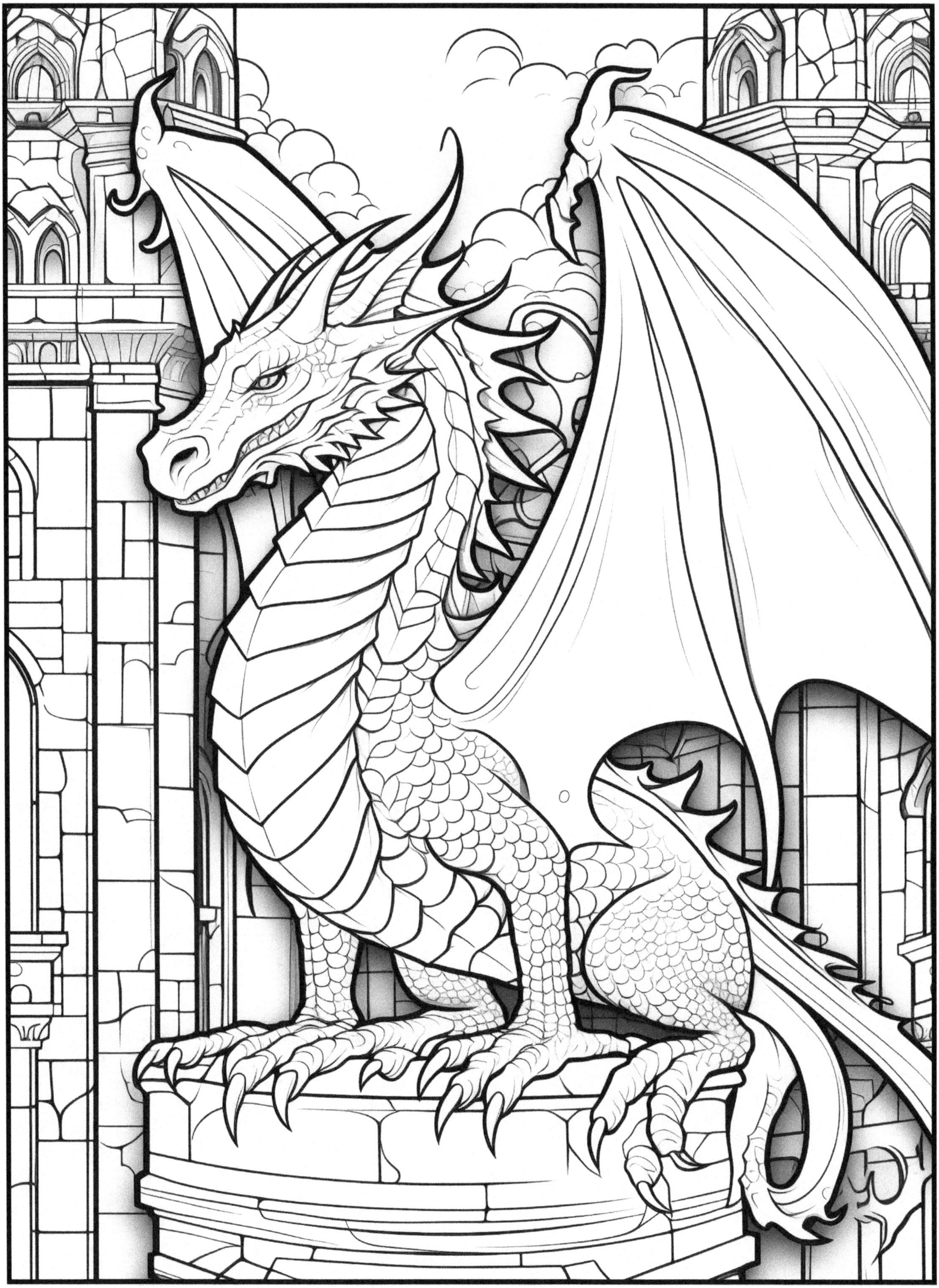

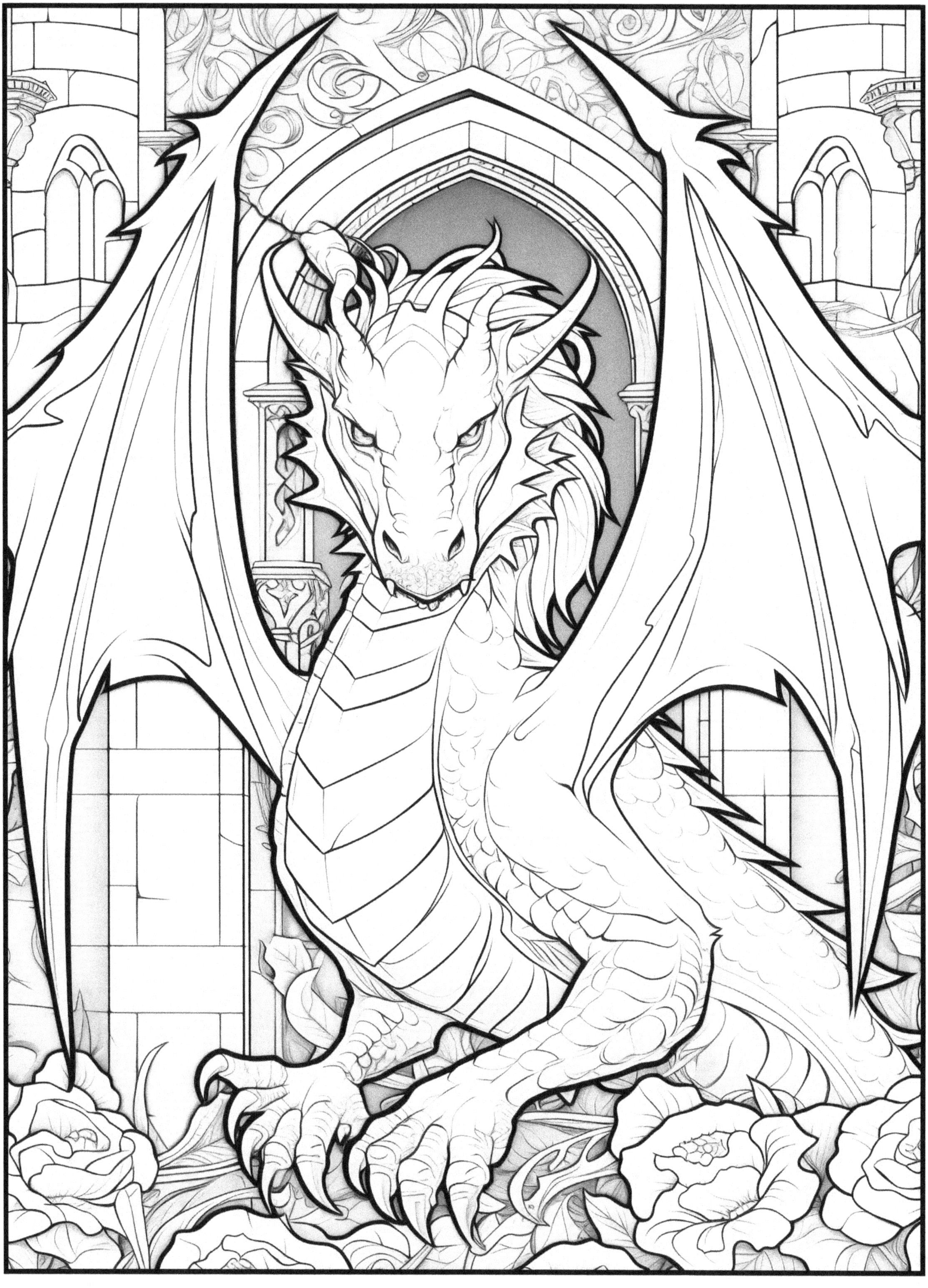

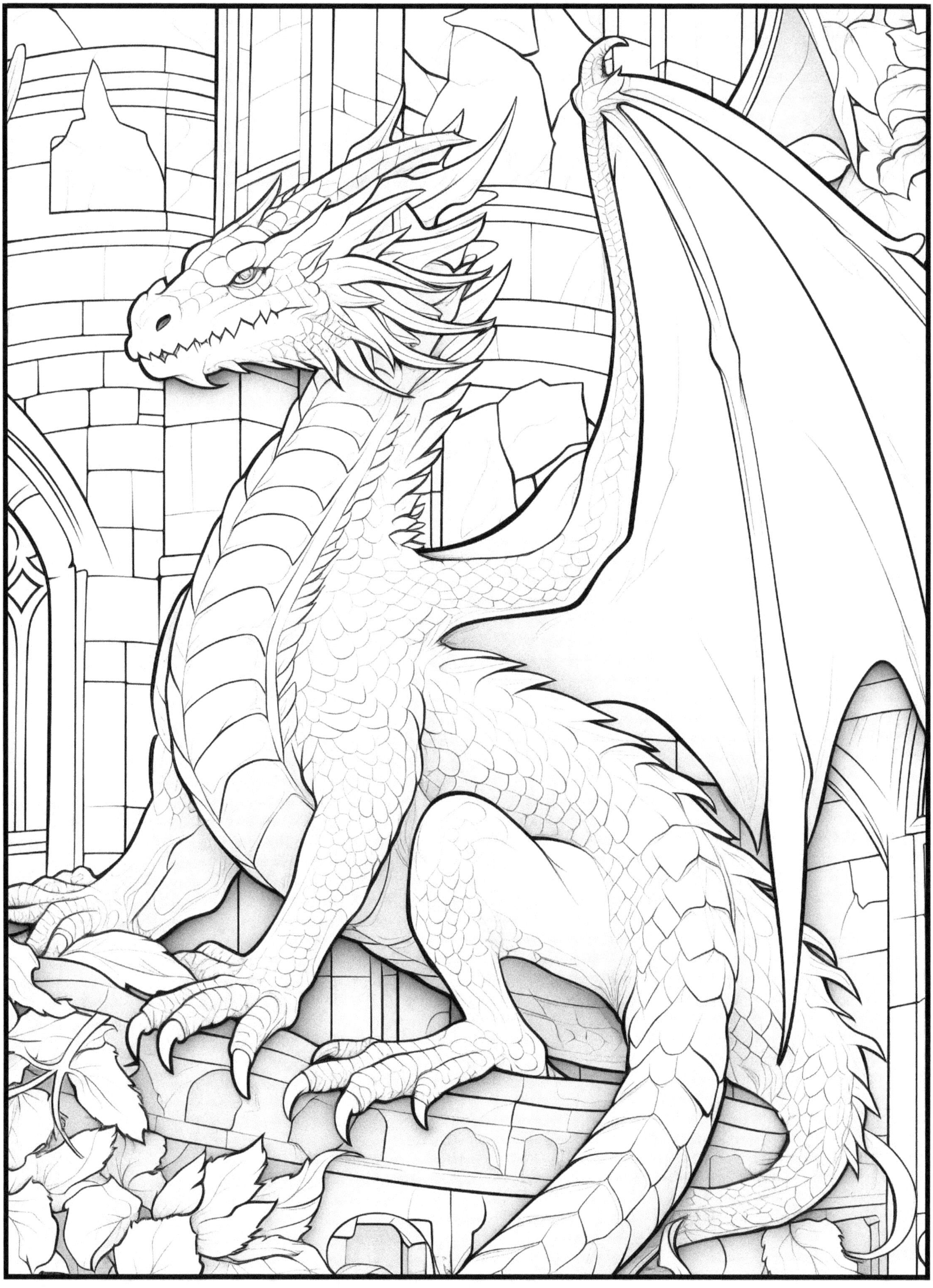

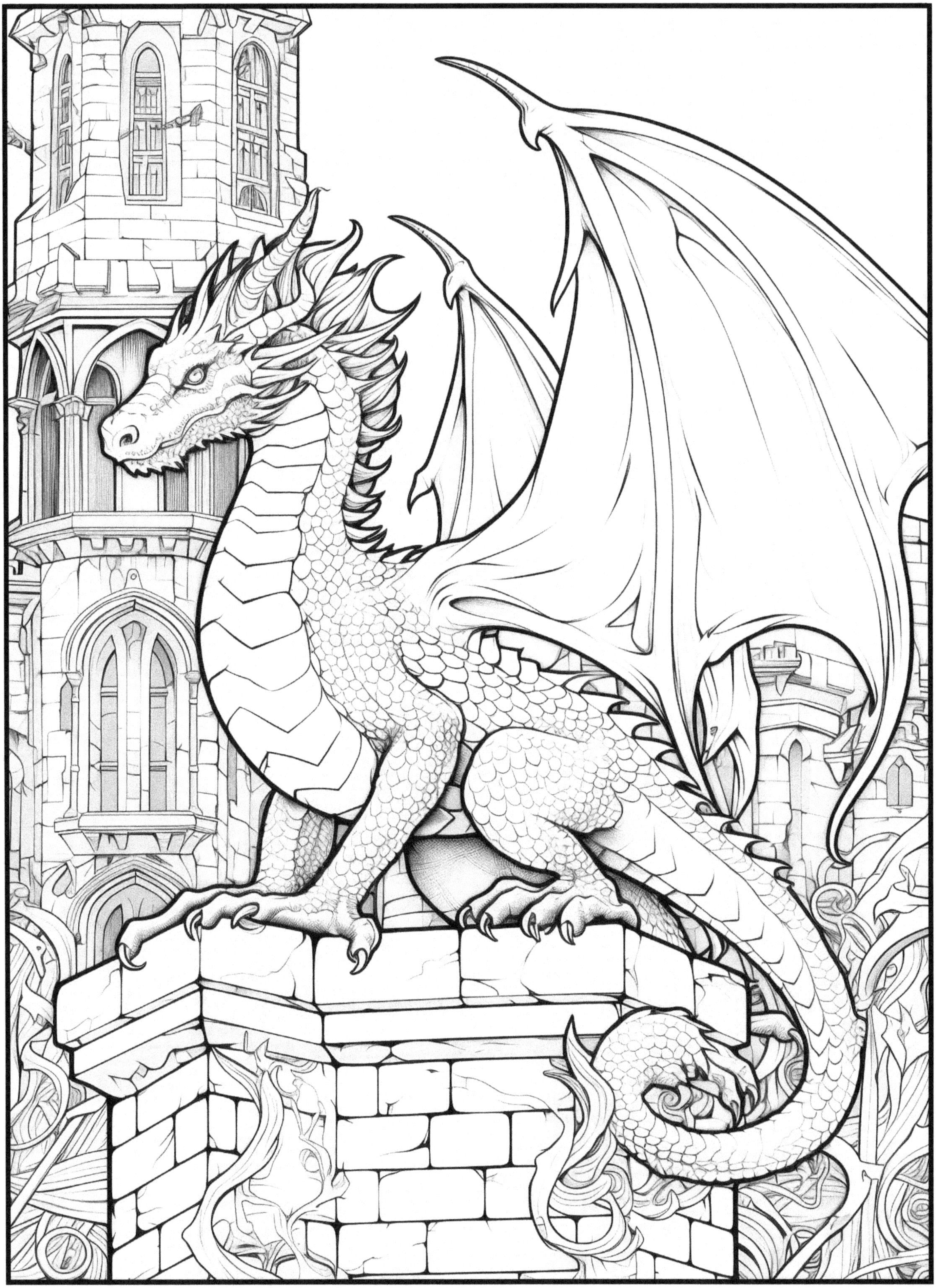

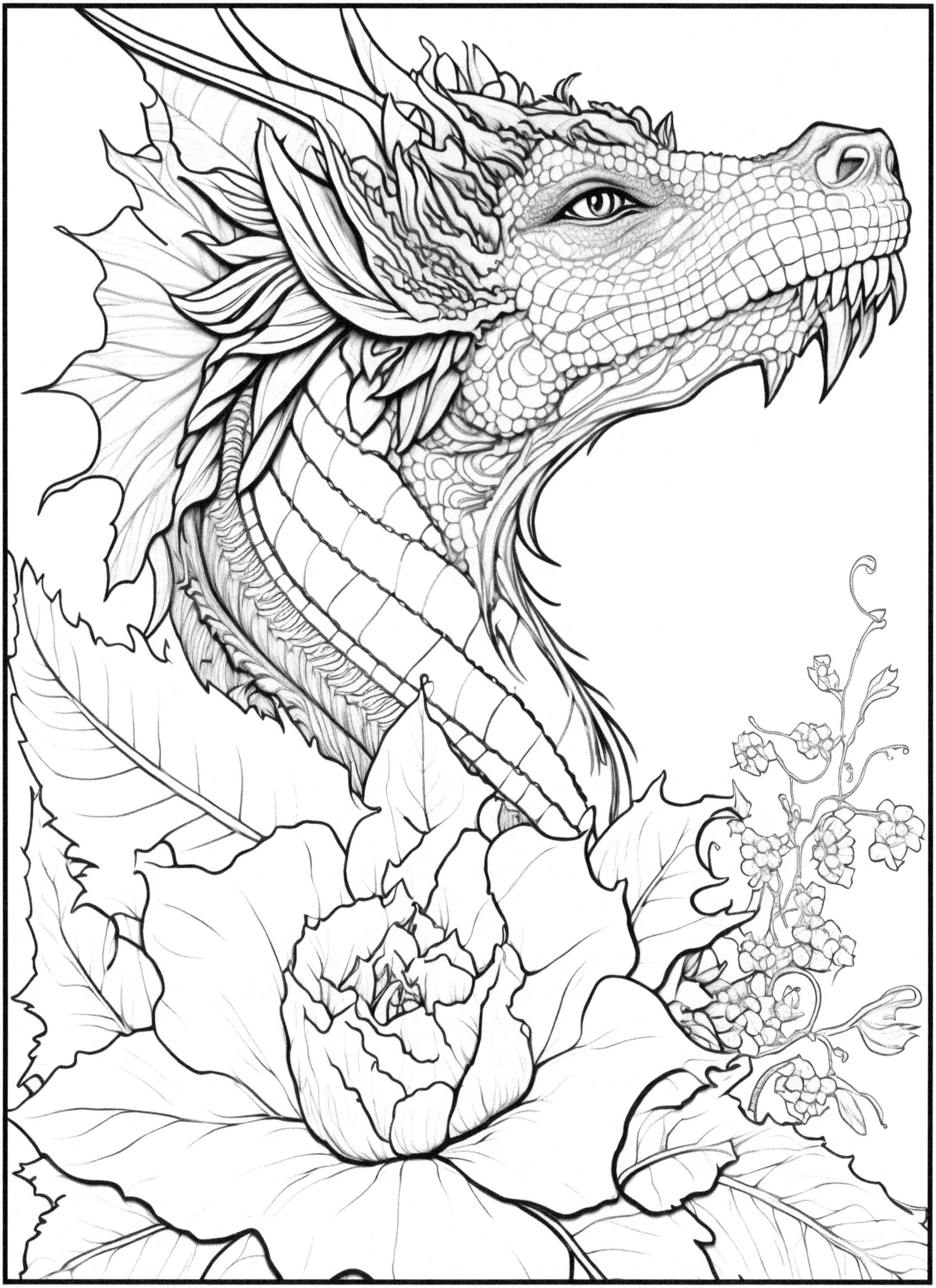

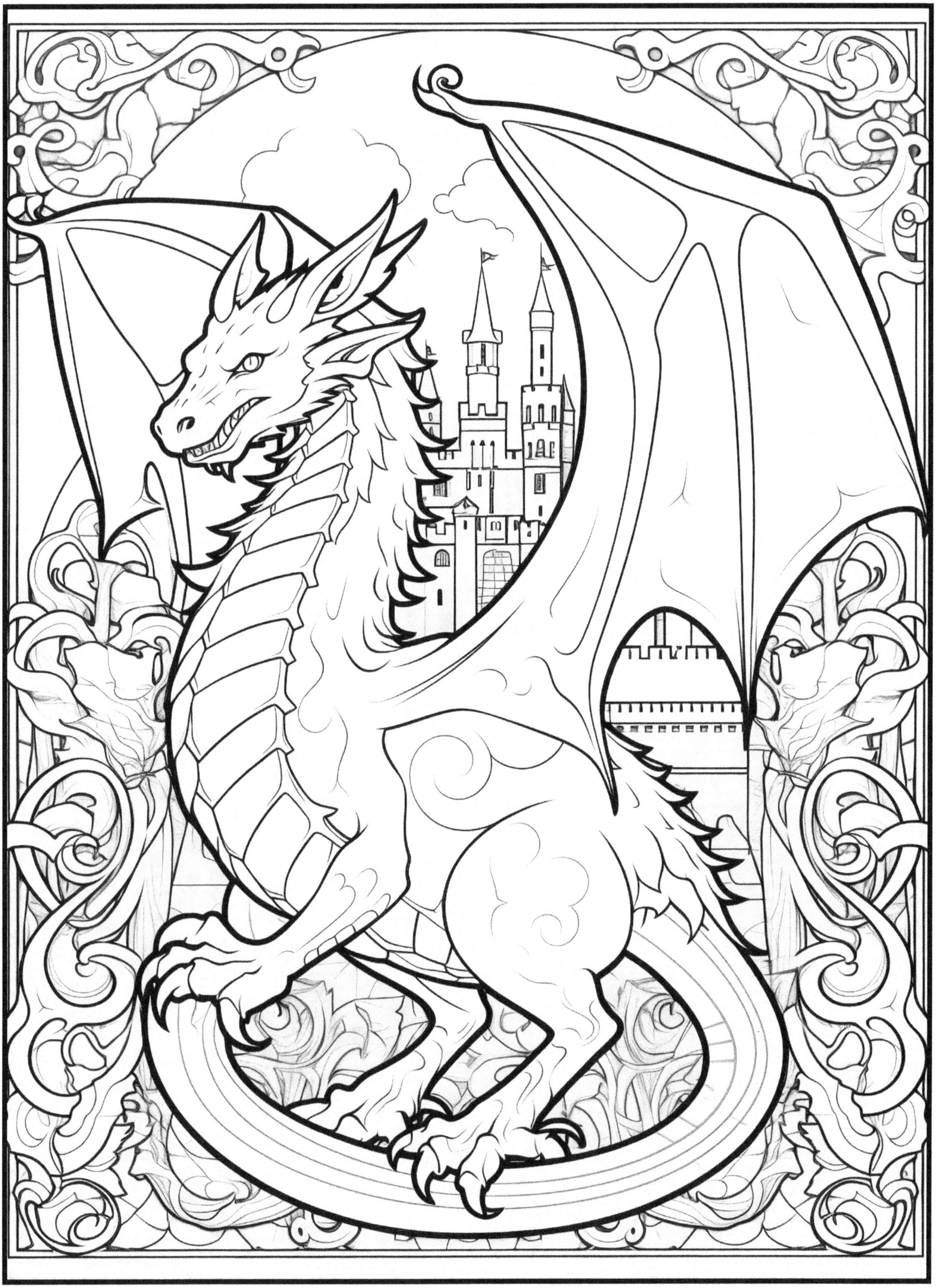

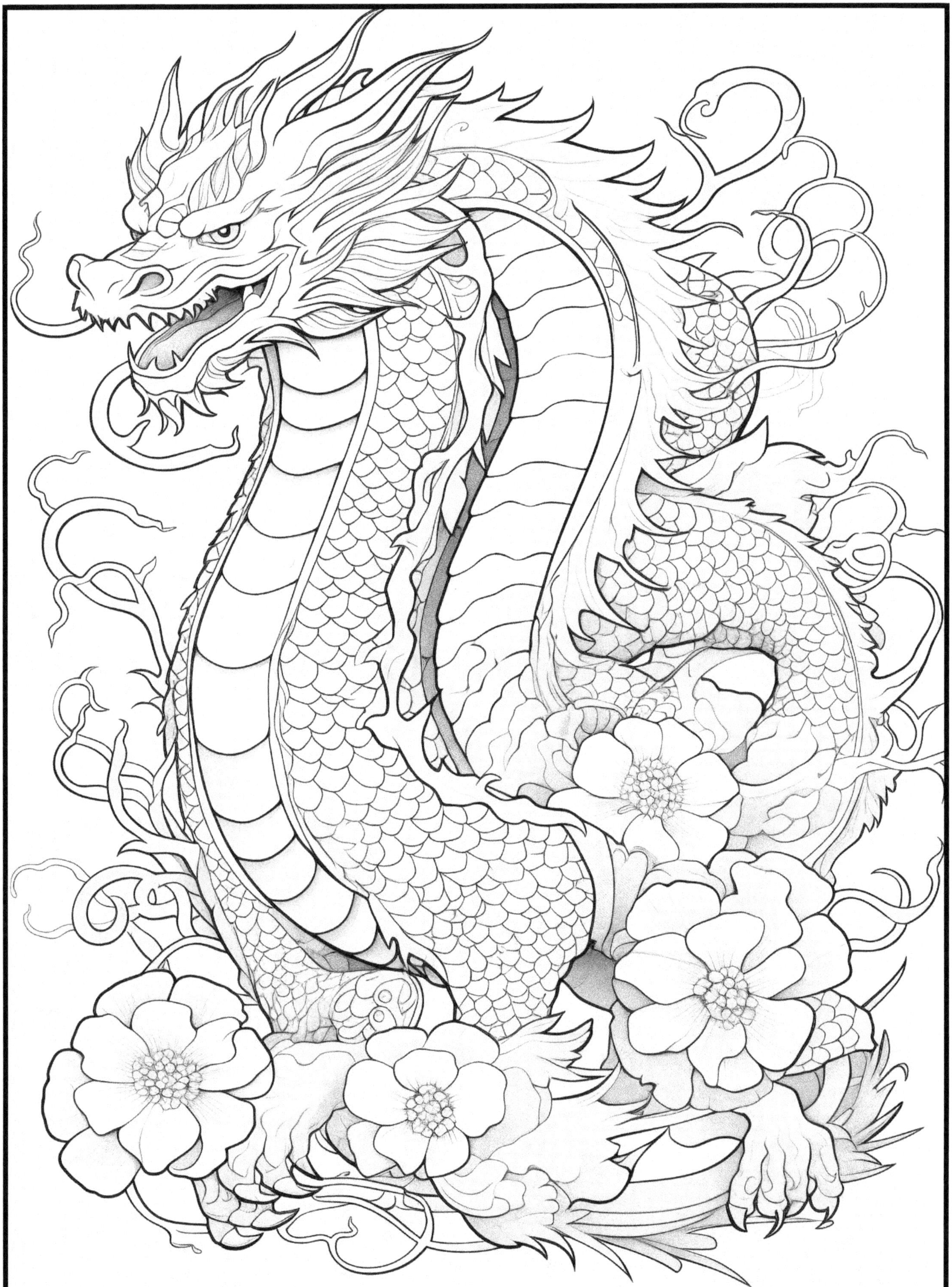

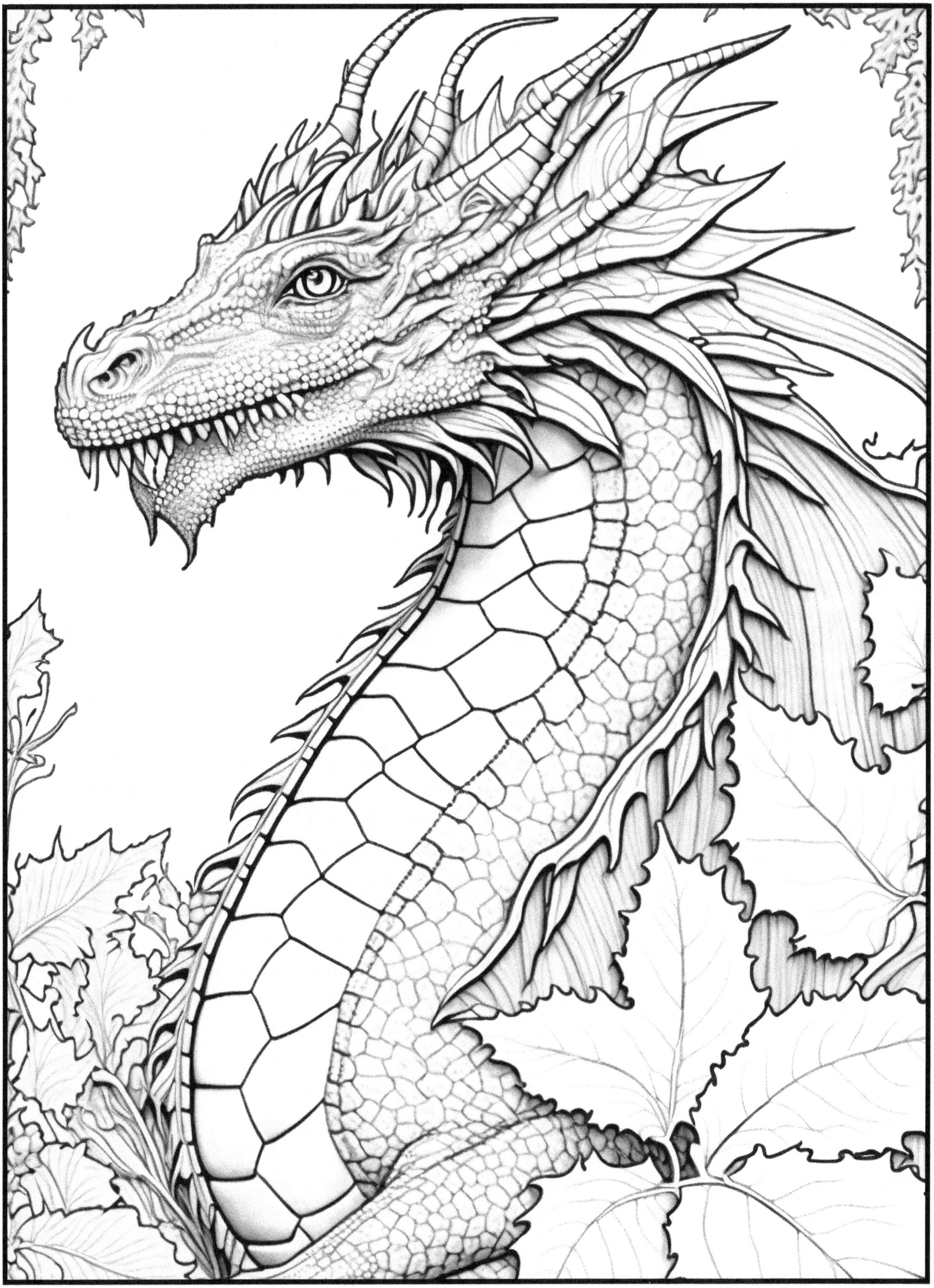

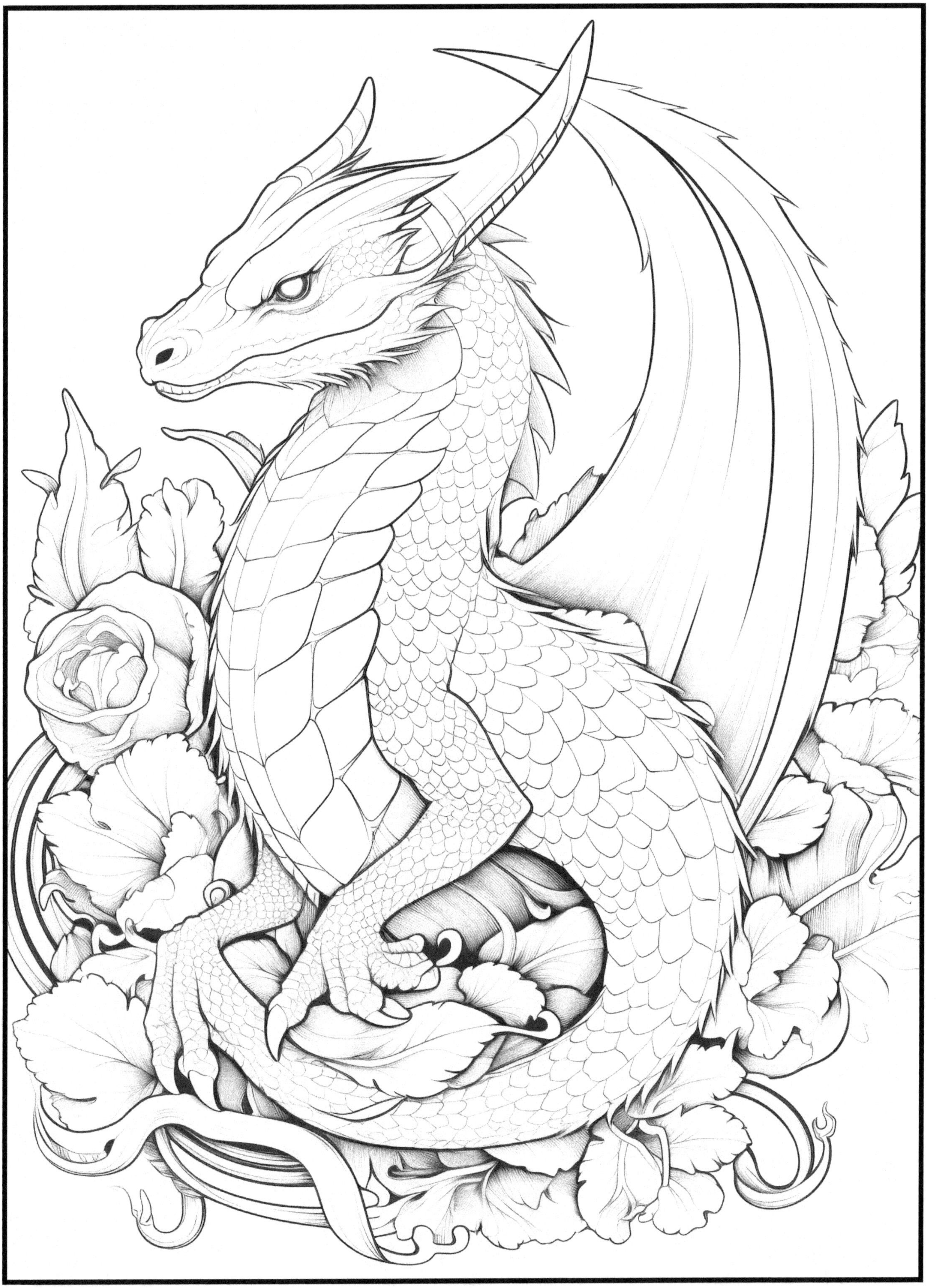

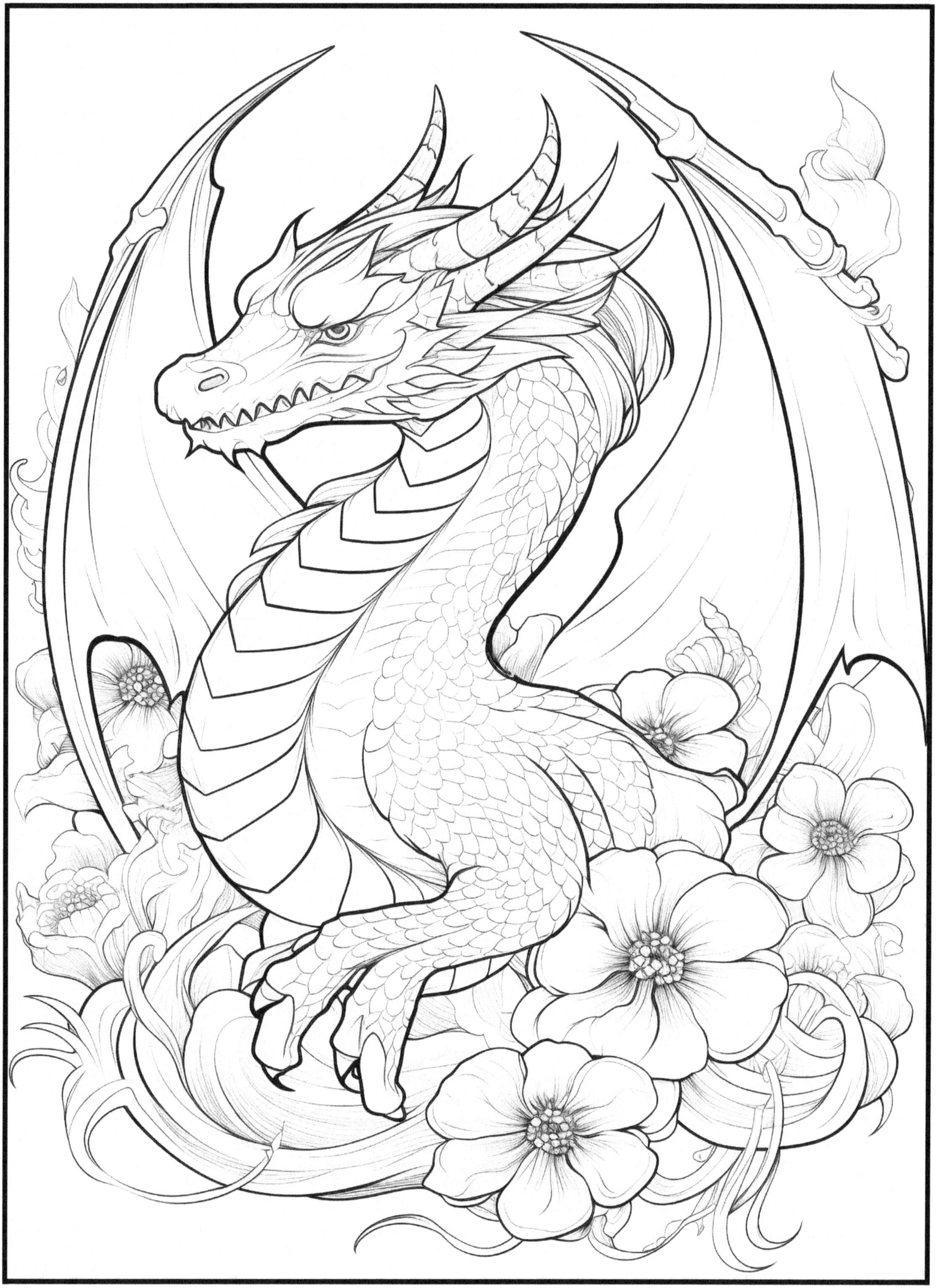

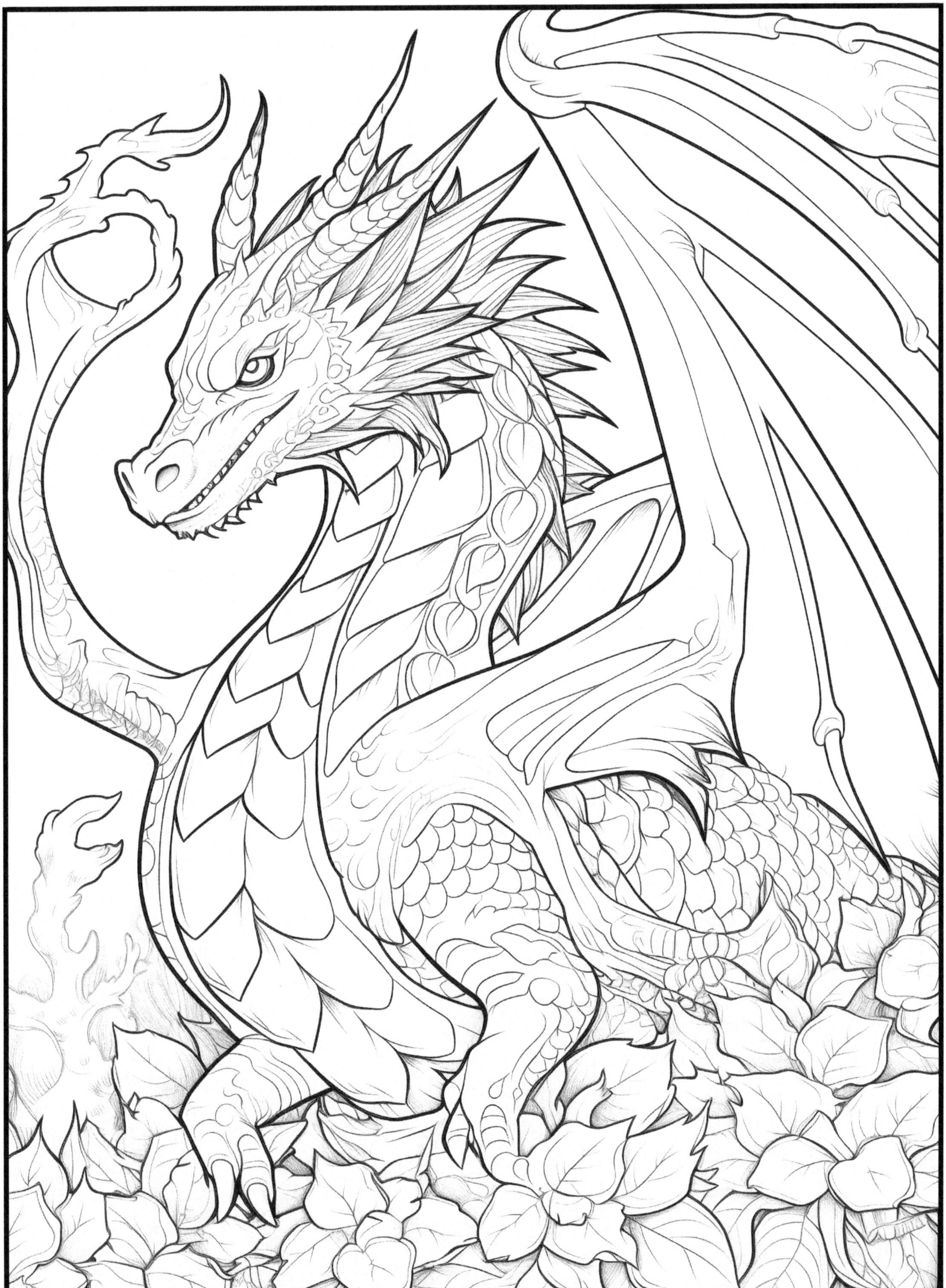

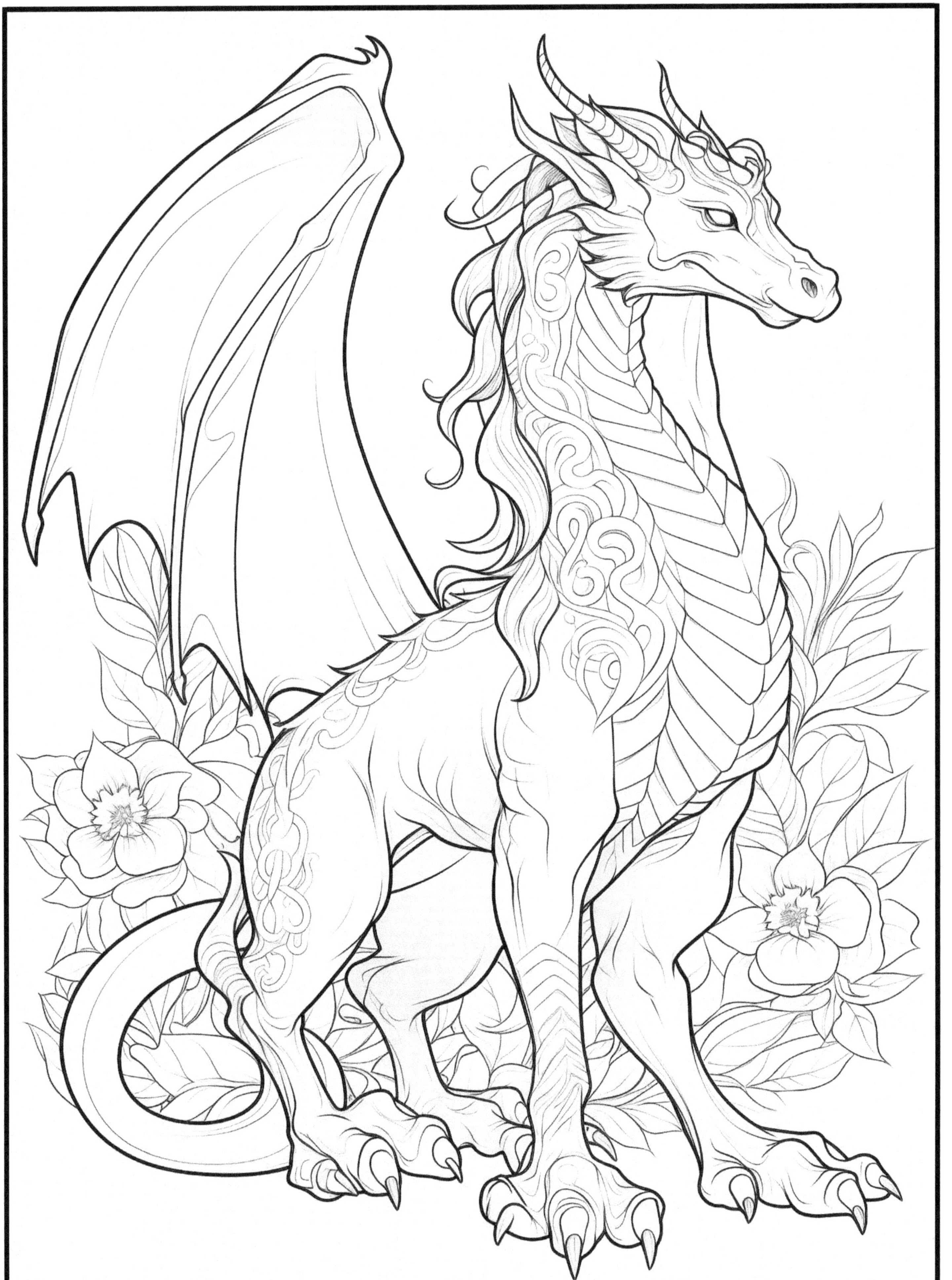

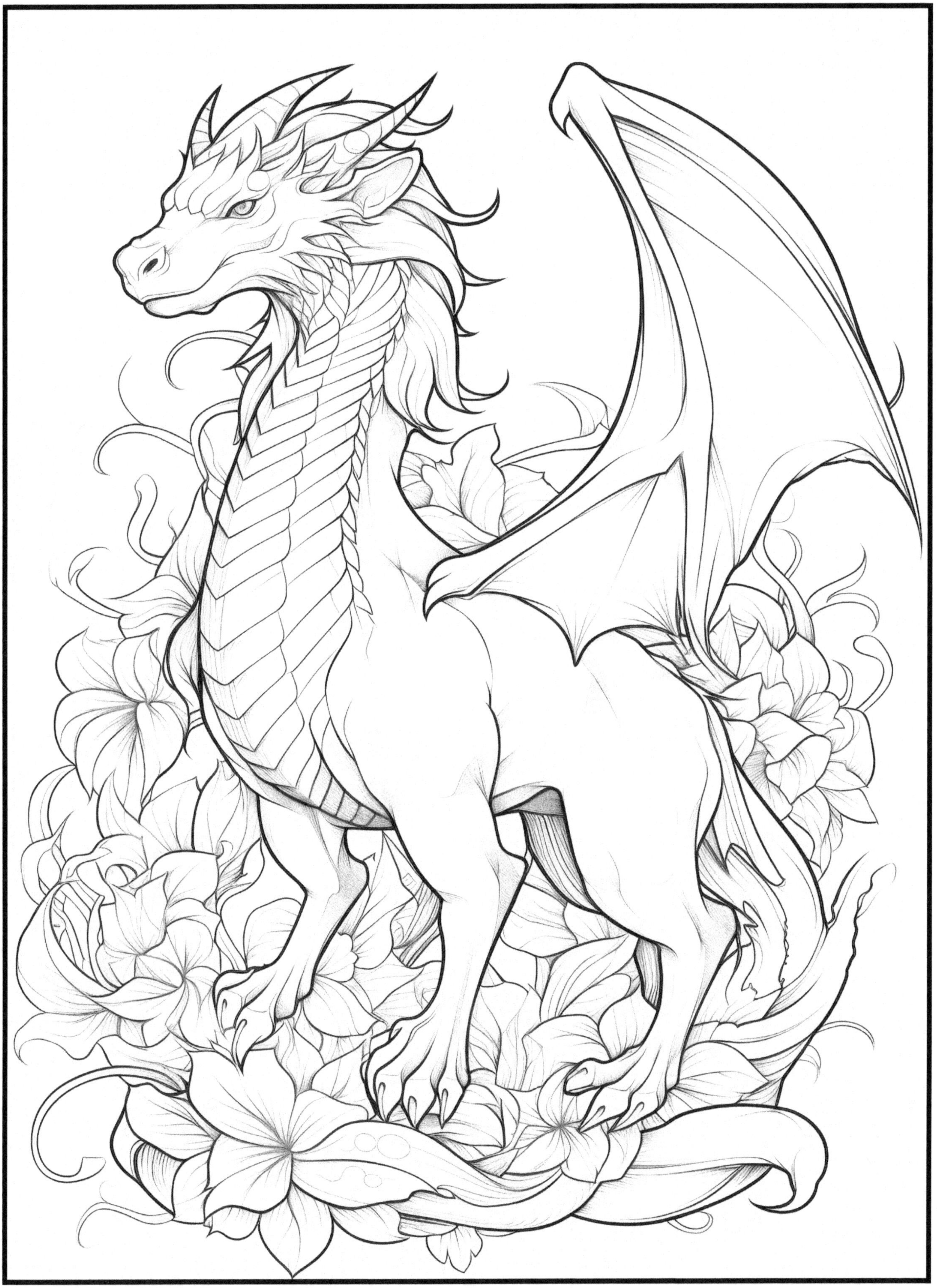

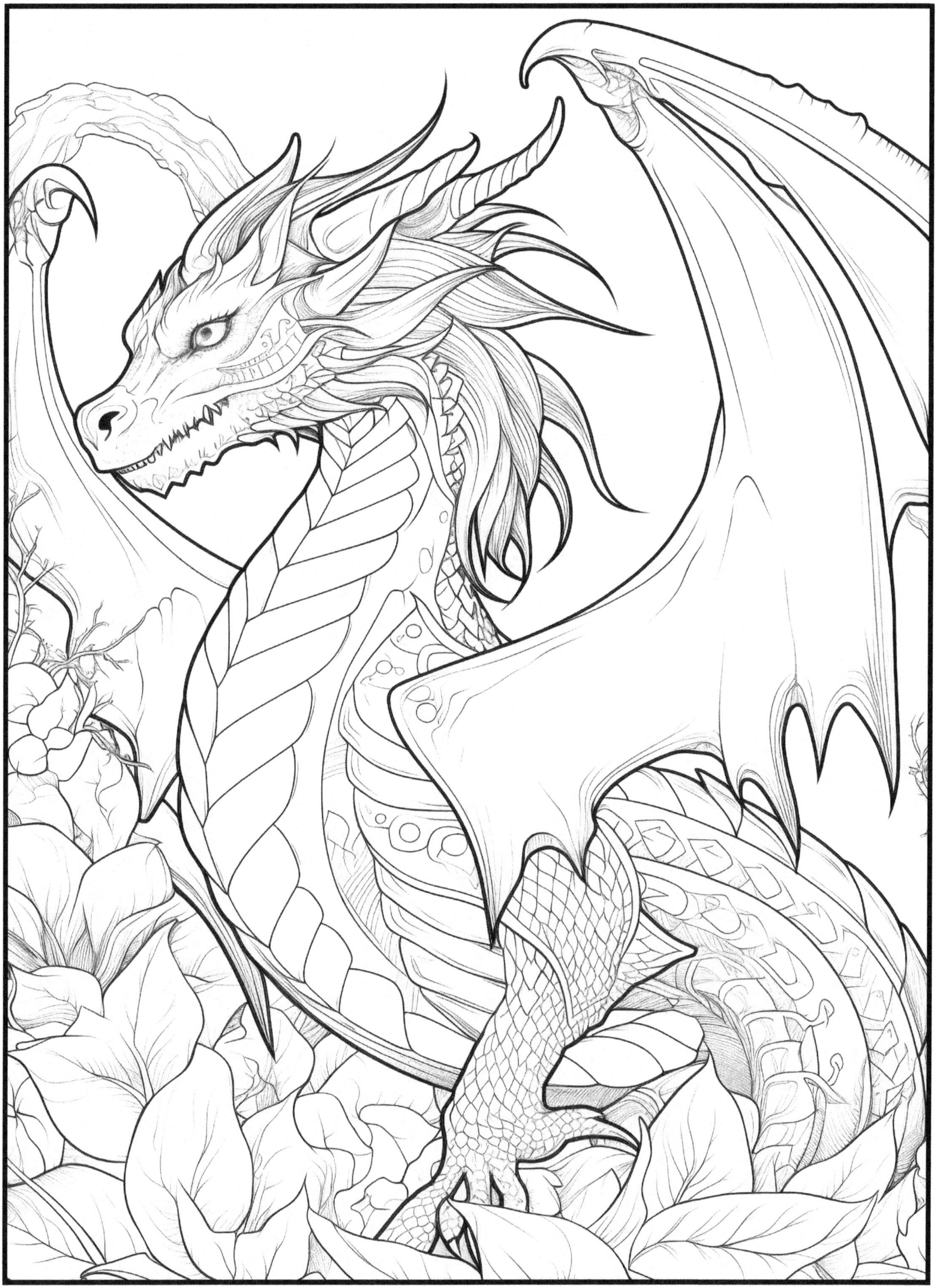

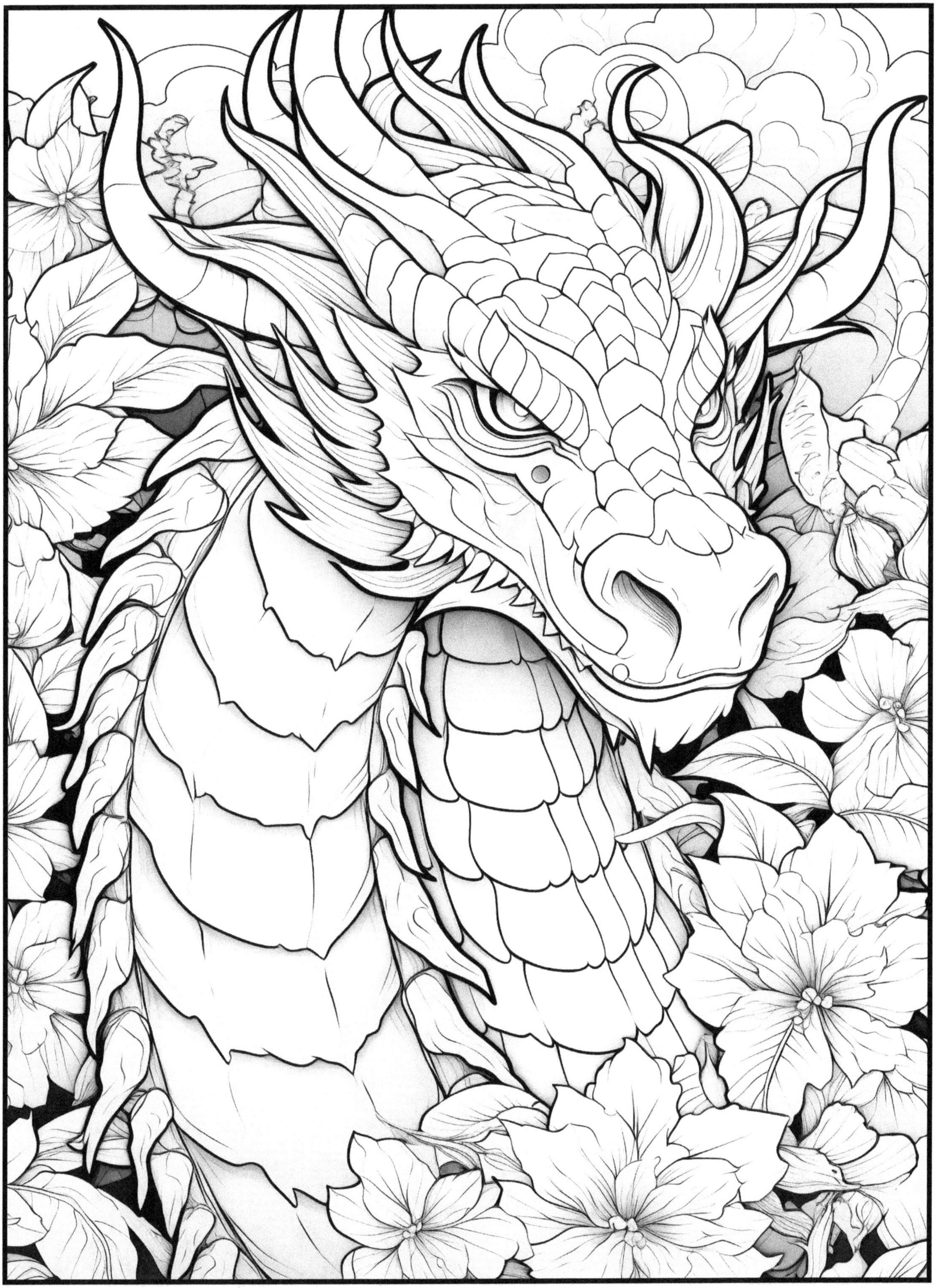

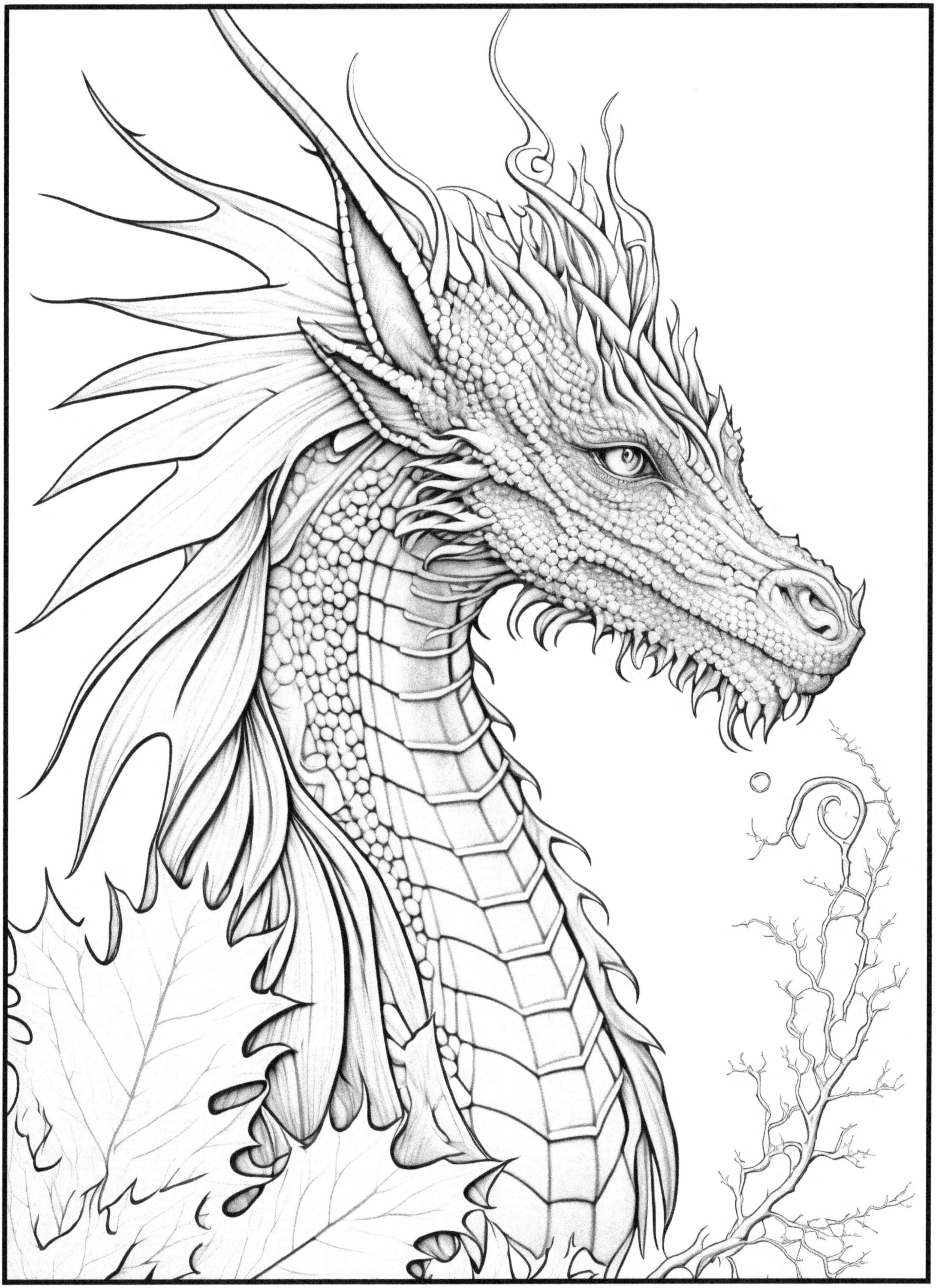

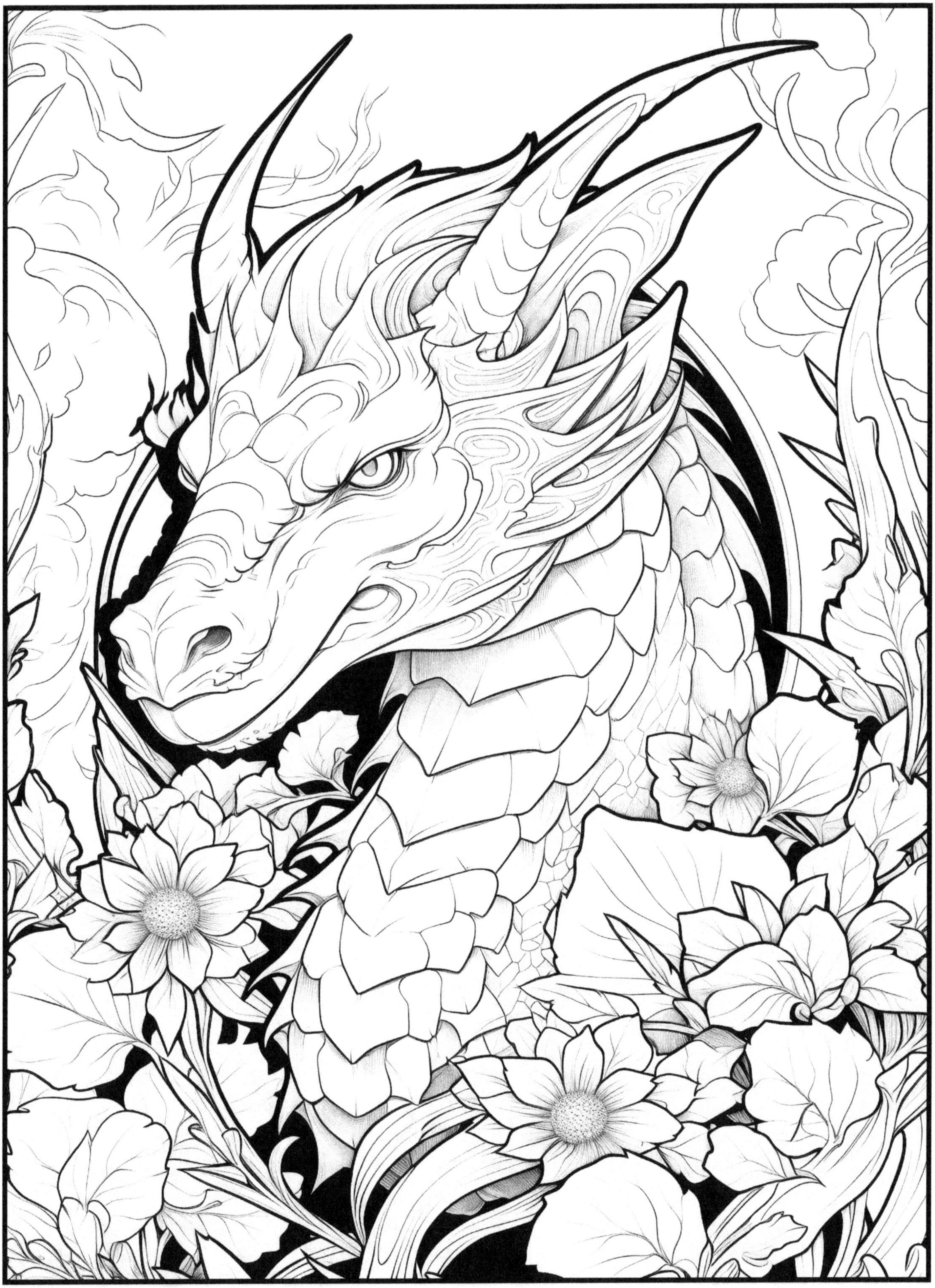

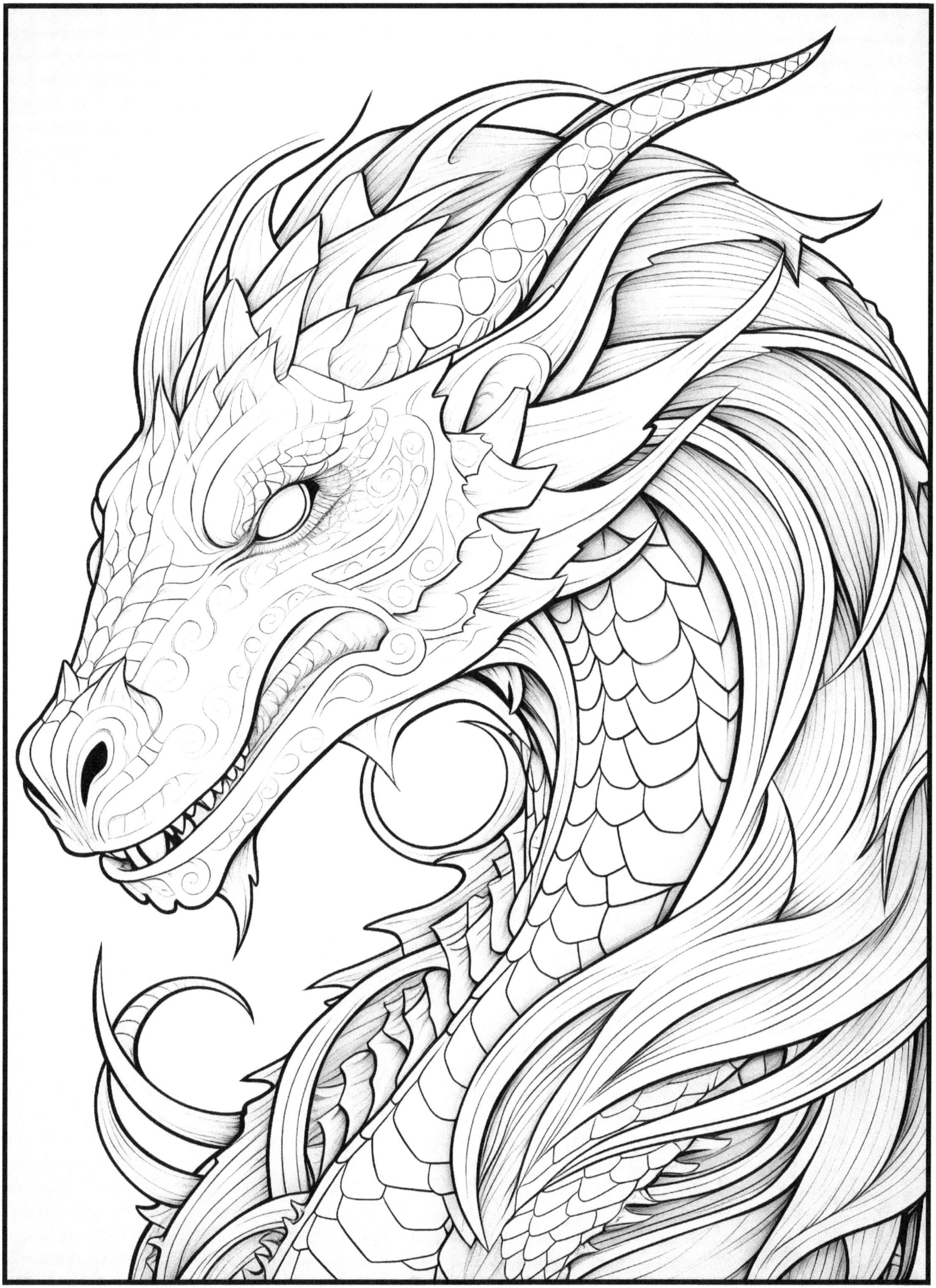

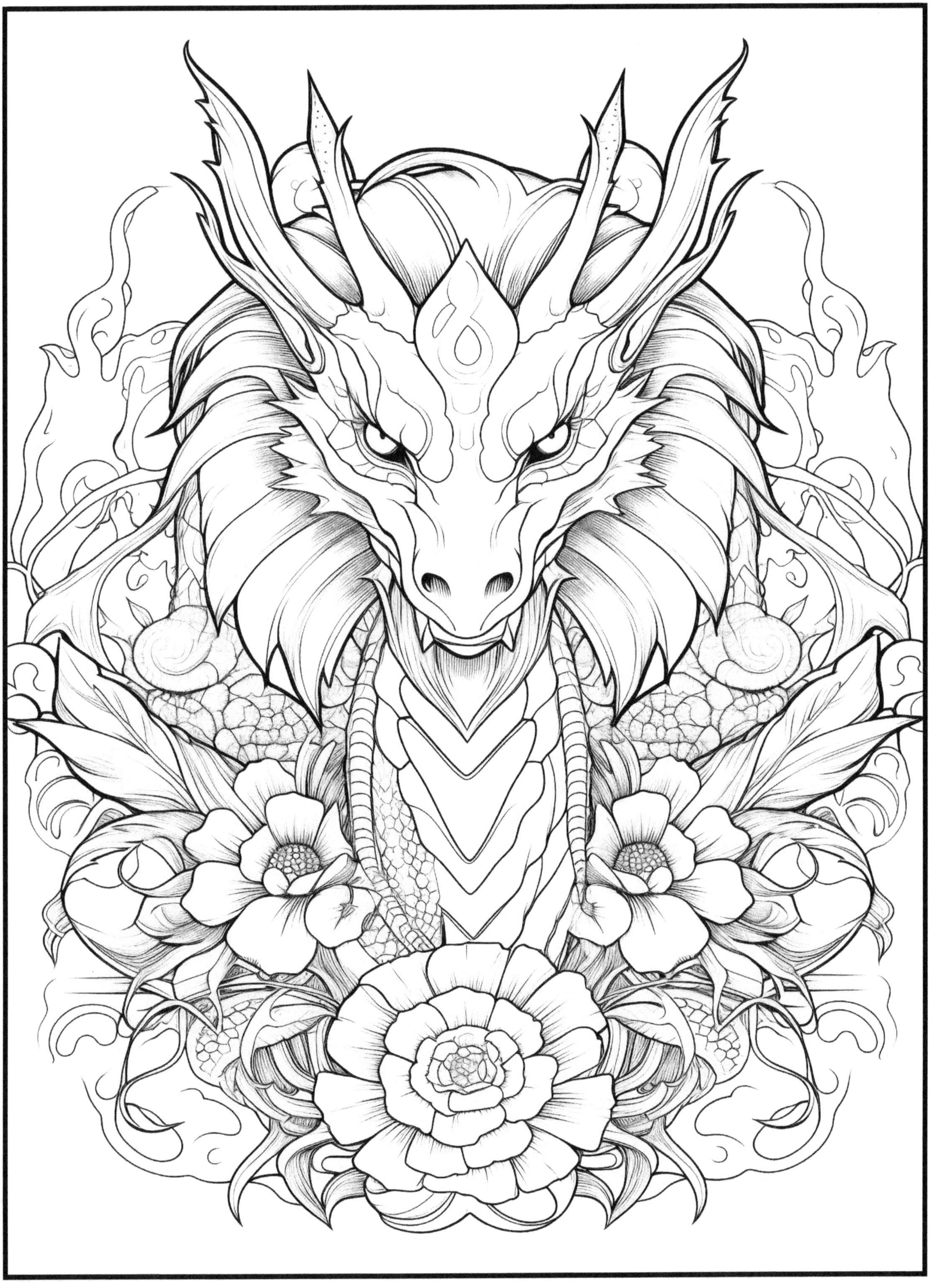

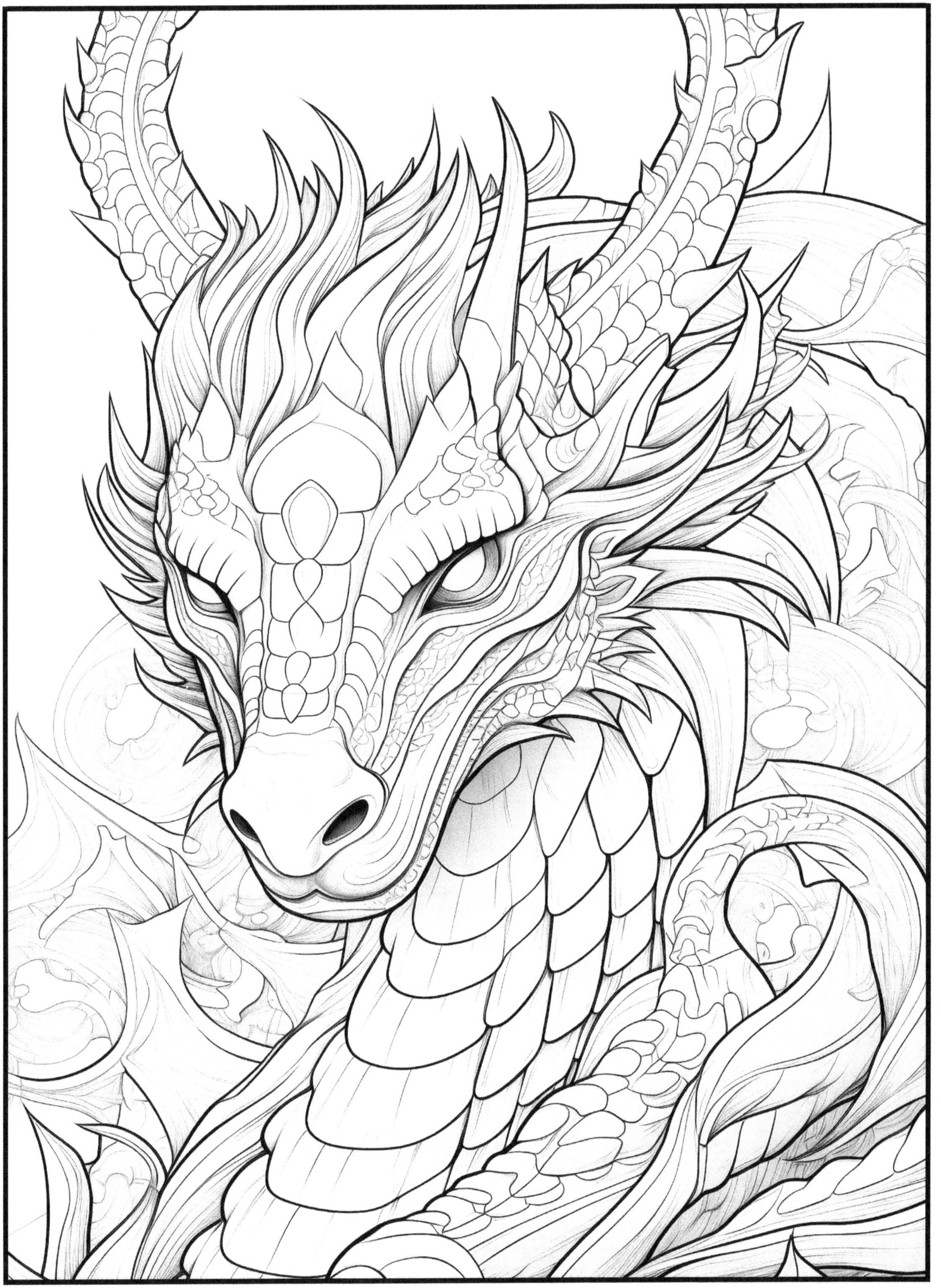

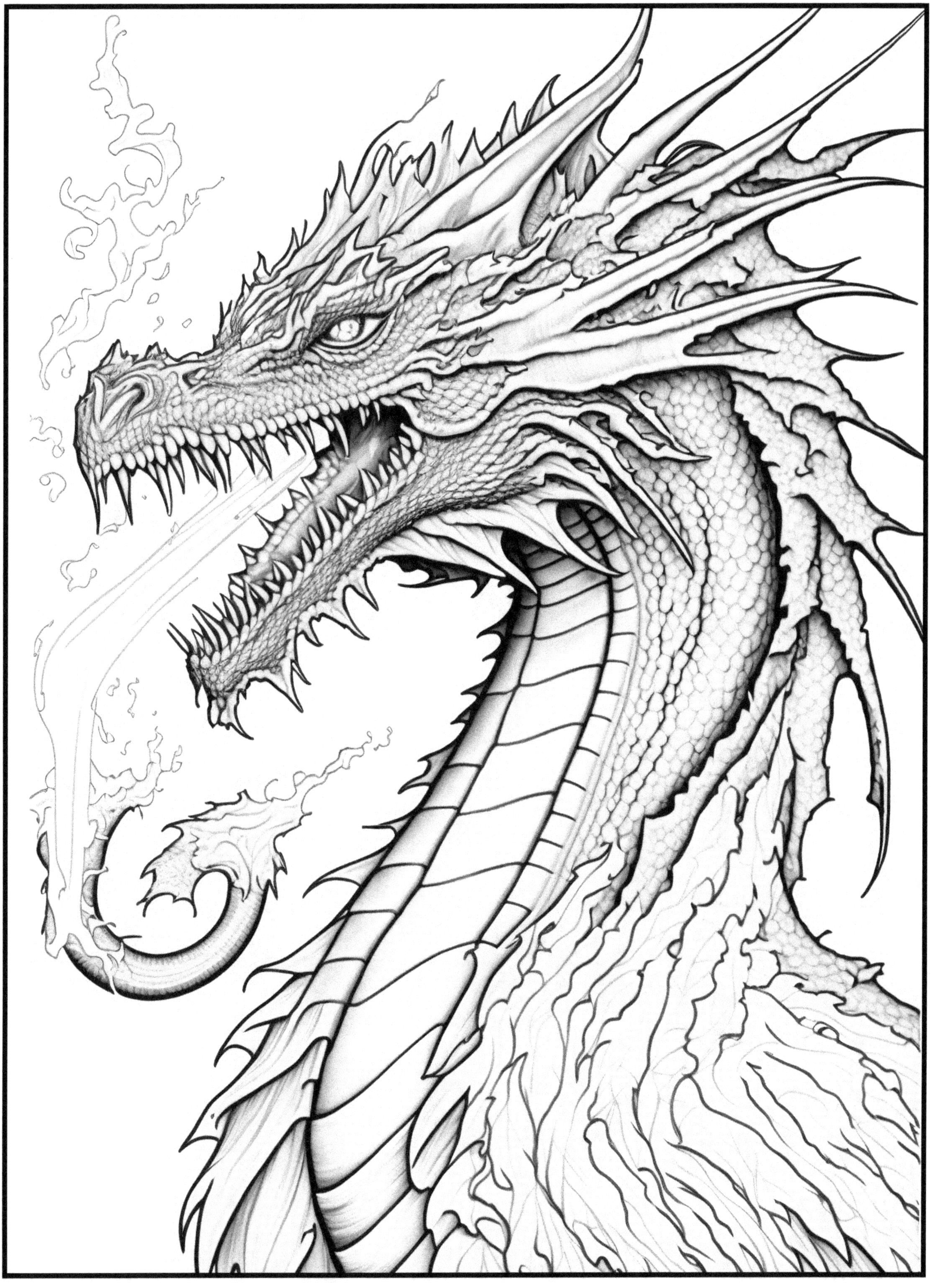

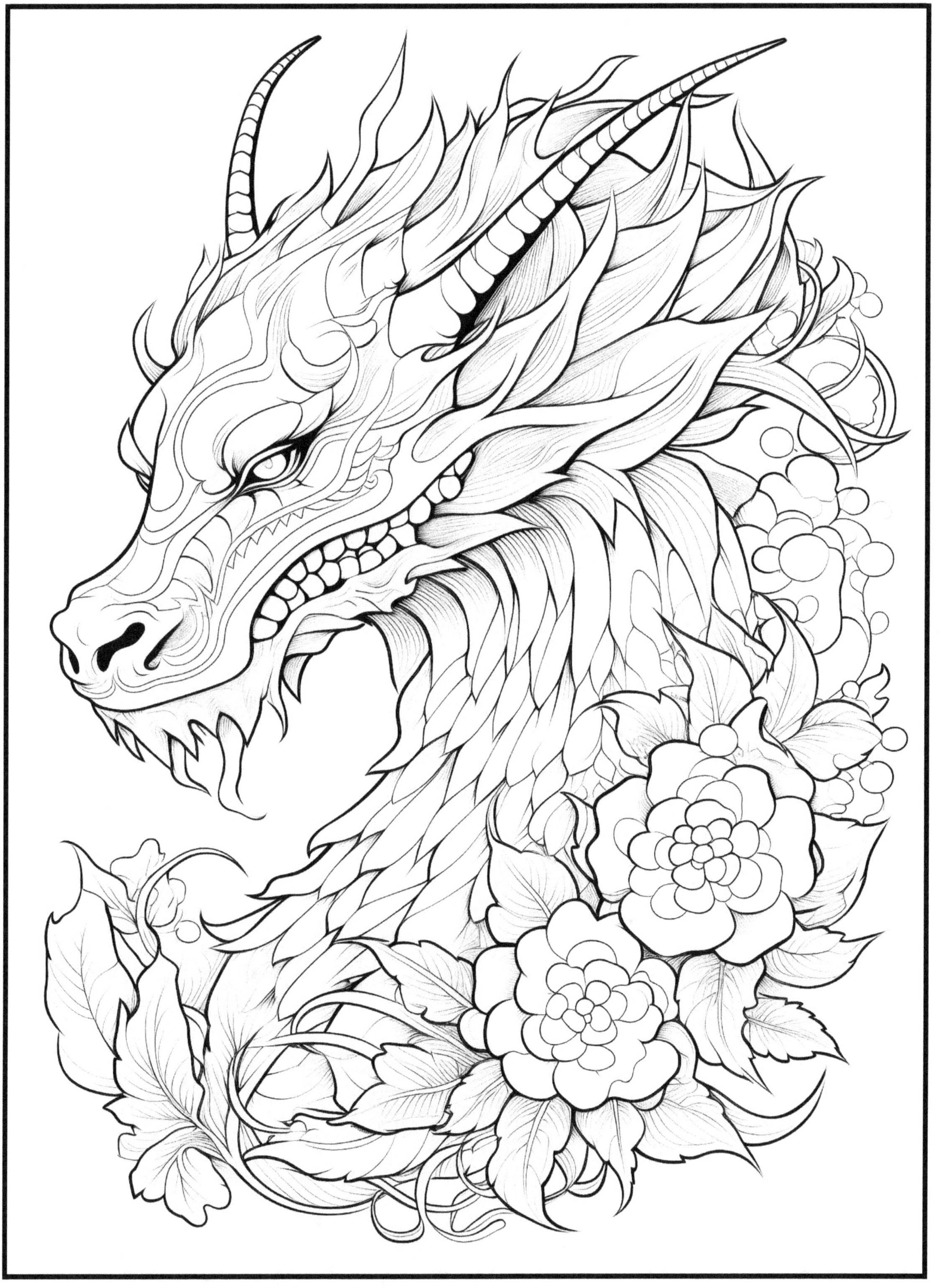

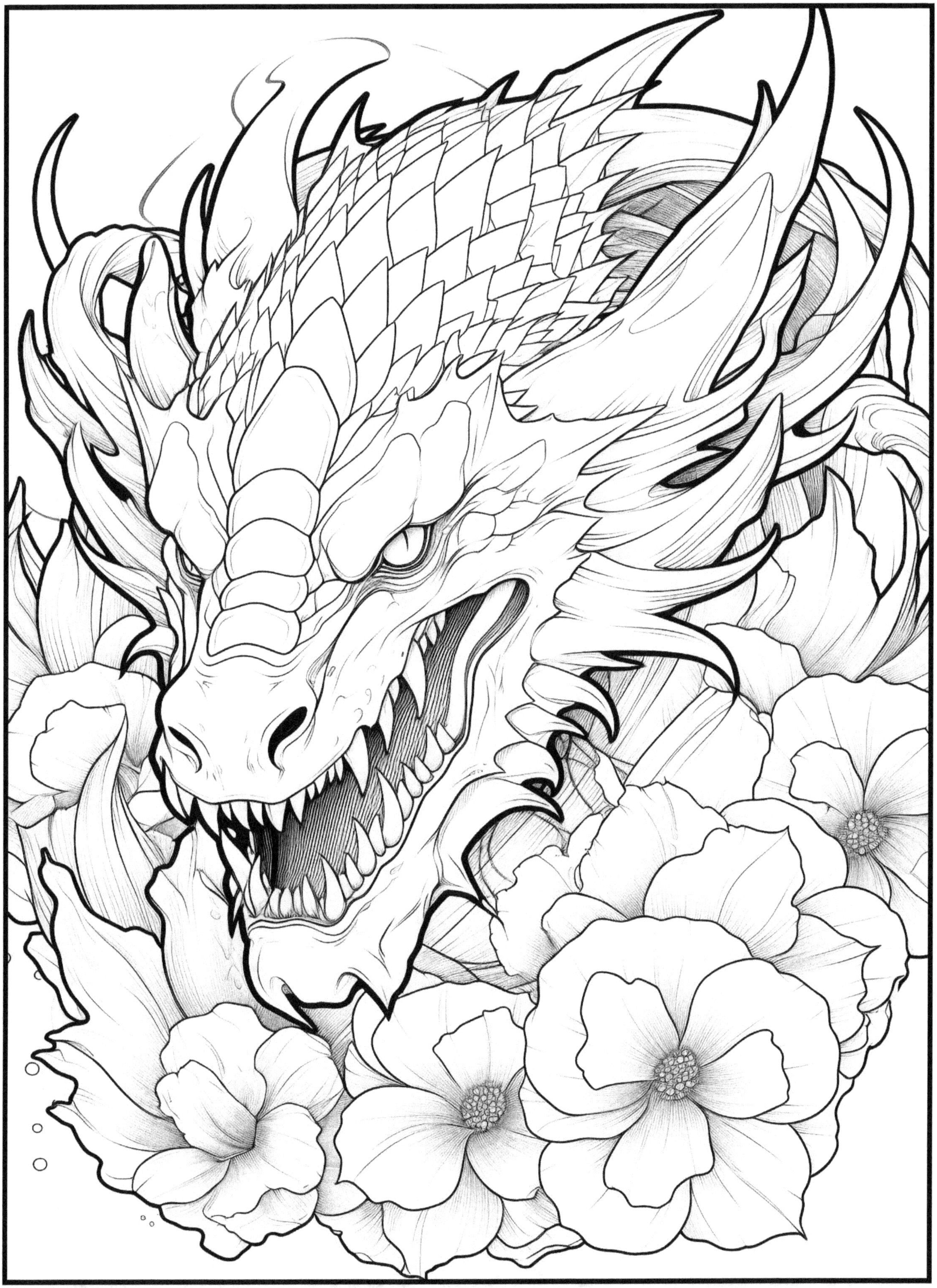

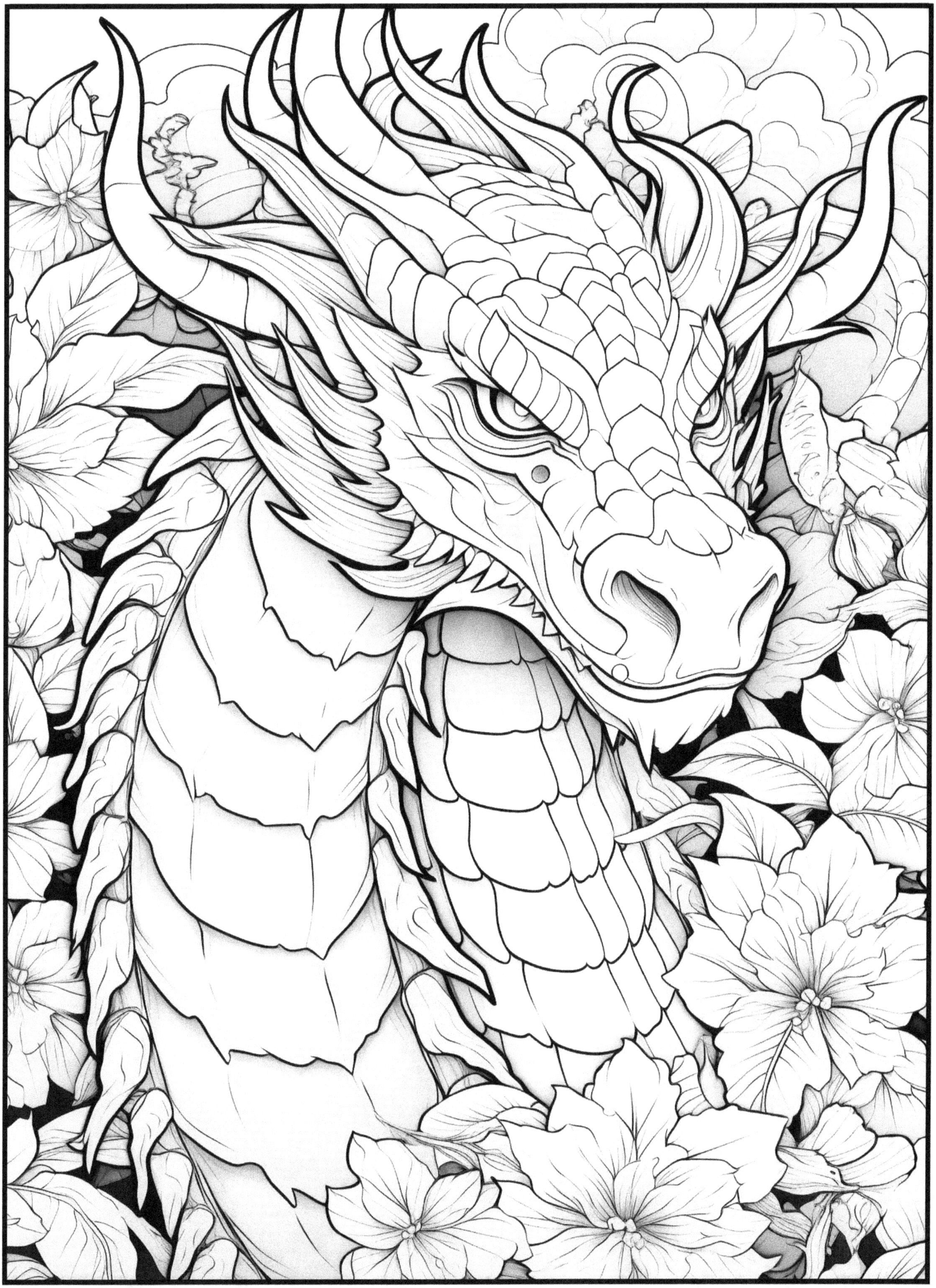

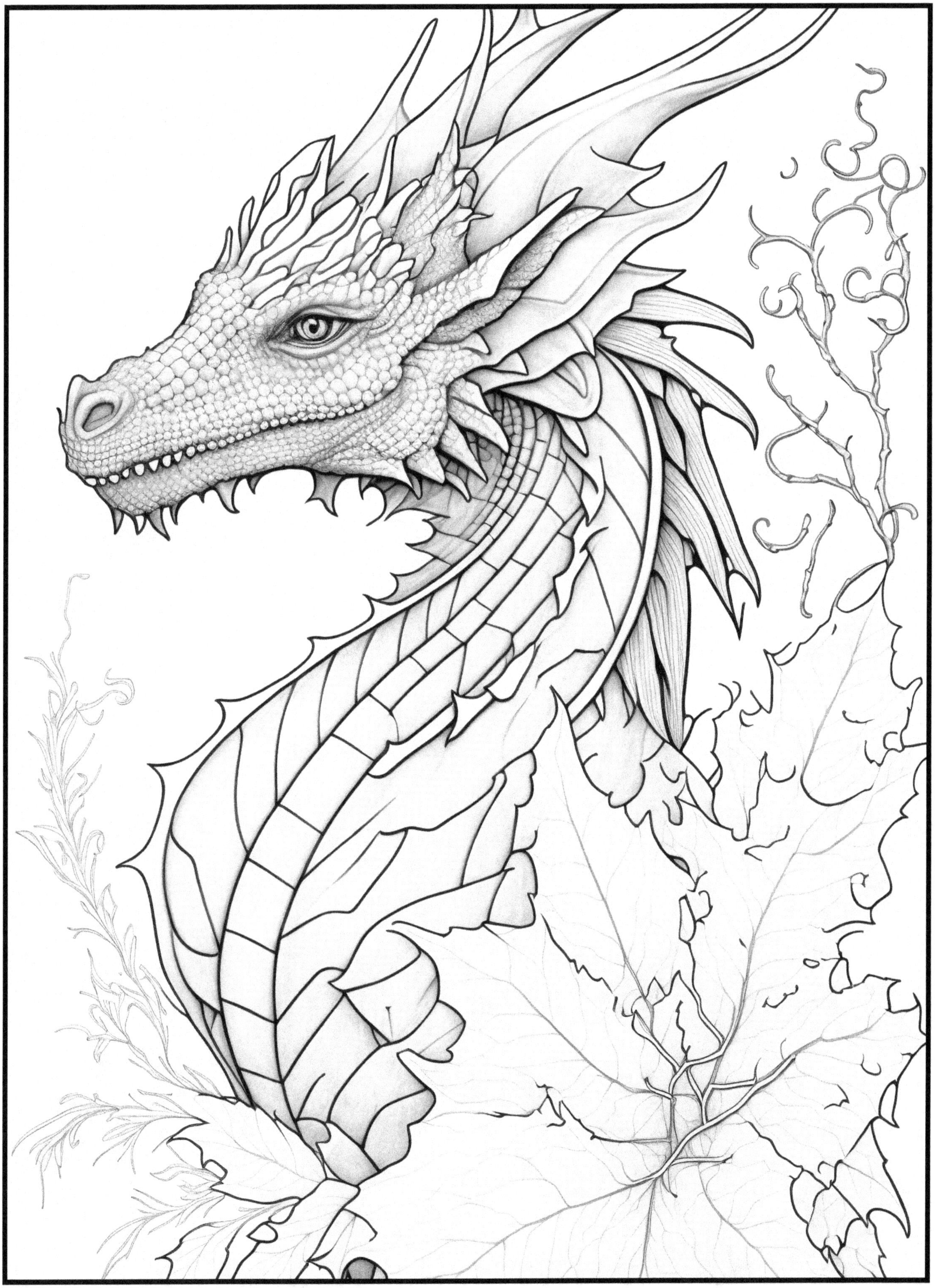

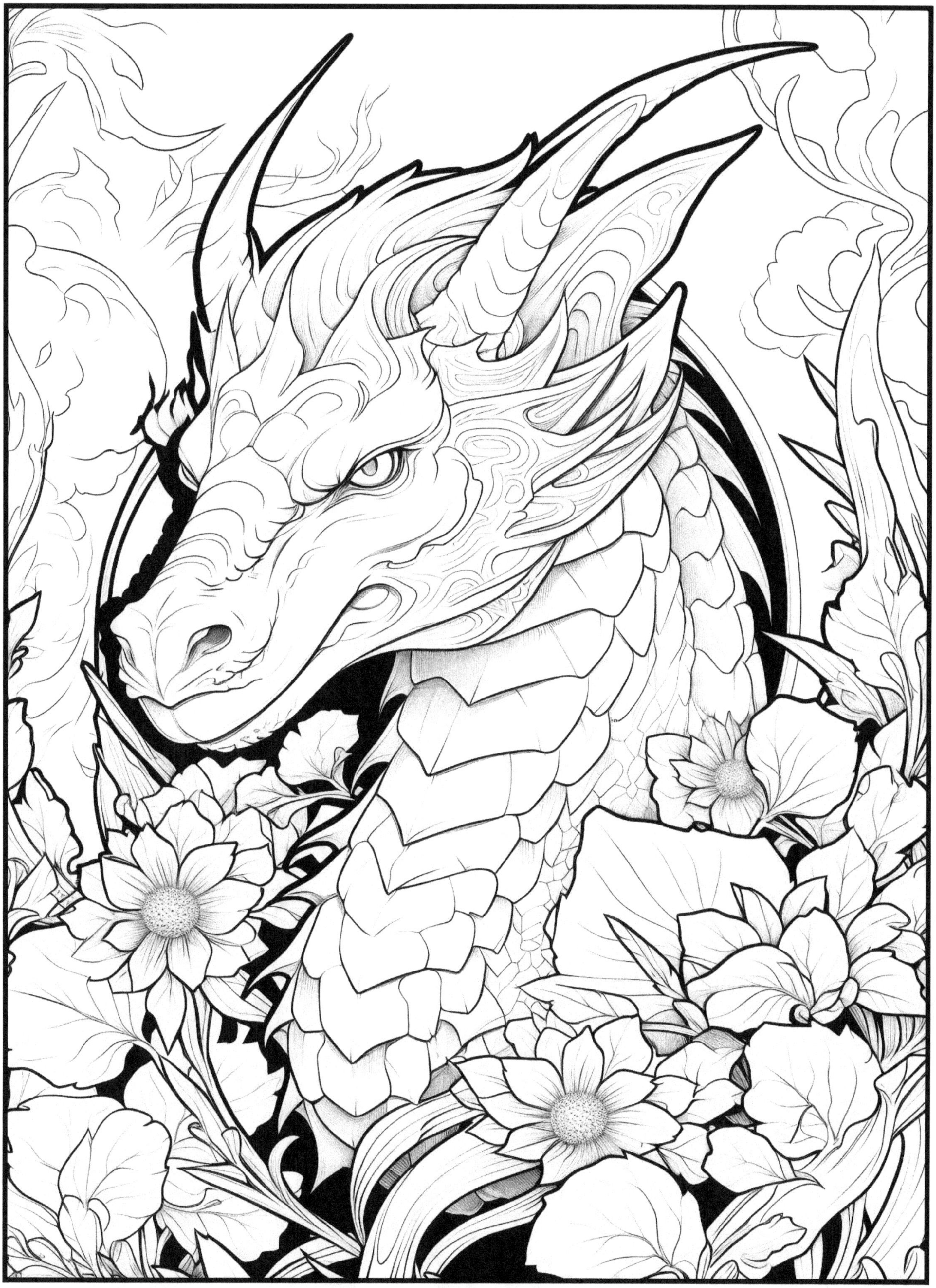

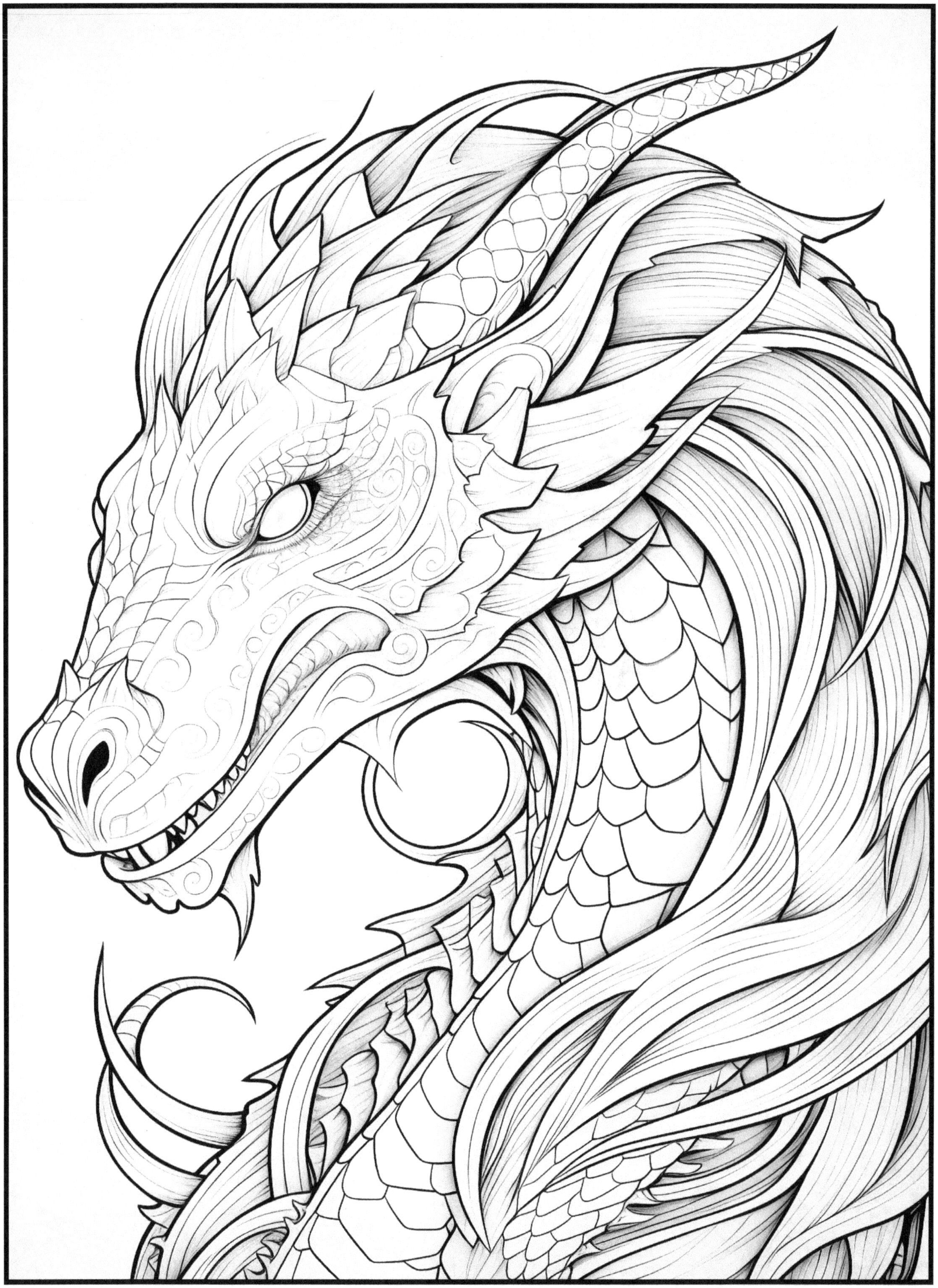

Did you enjoy this dragon adult coloring book?

If so please take a second to leave a review! A review is like gold-dust to independent artists like me! Thanks so much!

www.ingramcontent.com/pod-product-compliance
Lightning Source LLC
Chambersburg PA
CBHW080844220526
45467CB00008B/2389